Cultivation
of Christian
Character

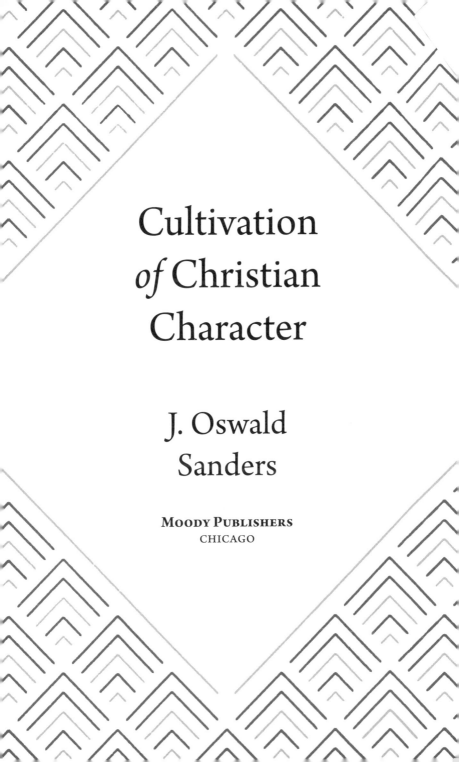

Cultivation *of* Christian Character

J. Oswald Sanders

MOODY PUBLISHERS
CHICAGO

Published by special arrangement with Discovery House, 3000 Kraft Avenue SE, Grand Rapids, Michigan 49512, USA.

All Scripture quotations, unless otherwise indicated, are taken from the King James Version.

Scripture quotations marked ASV are taken from the American Standard Version.

Scripture quotations marked AMPC are taken from the Amplified® Bible (AMPC), copyright © 1954, 1958, 1962, 1964, 1965, 1987 by The Lockman Foundation. Used by permission. www.Lockman.org

Scripture quotations marked NEB are taken from the New English Bible, copyright © 1961 by Cambridge University Press and Oxford University Press, 1961, 1970. All rights reserved.

Scripture quotations marked WILLIAMS N.T. are taken from Charles B. Williams, *The New Testament: A Translation in the Language of the People* (Boston: Bruce Humphries Inc., 1937). Slightly revised in 1950 (Chicago: Moody Press).

Scripture quotations marked MOFFATT are from *The Bible: James Moffatt Translation*, Copyright © 1922, 1924, 1925, 1926, 1935 Harper Collins San Francisco, Copyright © 1950, 1952, 1953, 1954 James A. R. Moffatt.

Scripture quotations marked MLB are taken from *The Modern Language Bible: The New Berkeley Version in Modern English*, Copyright © 1945, 1959, 1969 by Zondervan Publishing House.

Scripture quotations marked RV are taken from the Revised Version.

All emphasis in Scripture has been added.

Interior and cover design: Erik M. Peterson
Cover pattern copyright © 2017 by Strawberry Blossom/iStock (865272260). All rights reserved.

Library of Congress Cataloging-in-Publication Data

Names: Sanders, J. Oswald (John Oswald), 1902-1992, author.
Title: Cultivation of Christian character / by J. Oswald Sanders.
Description: Chicago : Moody Press, [2019] | Originally published in 1965 | Identifiers: LCCN 2019003384 (print) | LCCN 2019008439 (ebook) | ISBN 9780802497628 () | ISBN 9780802418906
Subjects: LCSH: Spiritual formation. | Christian life.
Classification: LCC BV4511 (ebook) | LCC BV4511 .S26 2019 (print) | DDC 248.4--dc23
LC record available at https://lccn.loc.gov/2019003384

ISBN: 978-0-8024-1890-6

We hope you enjoy this book from Moody Publishers. Our goal is to provide high-quality, thought-provoking books and products that connect truth to your real needs and challenges. For more information on other books and products written and produced from a biblical perspective, go to www.moodypublishers. com or write to:

Moody Publishers
820 N. LaSalle Boulevard
Chicago, IL 60610

1 3 5 7 9 10 8 6 4 2

Printed in the United States of America

Contents

Introduction

The genuine disciple of Christ earnestly desires a closer walk with God and a greater conformity to Christ. If these are absent, there is reason to doubt the genuineness of the discipleship. But many true lovers of the Lord are beset with a sense of inadequacy and failure in living the Christian life as it ought to be lived. They are very conscious with Paul that they have not already attained, neither are already perfect, but they yearn to know Christ better and serve Him more worthily.

It is to such that this little volume is addressed. Some chapters are devoted to a diagnosis of the spiritual ailments which may be causing failure, others to prescribing the appropriate scriptural remedy. Some highlight the spiritual forces that oppose the Christian as he presses forward in the warfare with evil, others unfold the way of victory, a victory won on the Cross for all believers and made available to all by the Holy Spirit. It is a victory entered upon by faith, and maintained by continued faith, nourished by devout meditation on the Word and the practice of prayer. May the message be mixed with faith in those who read it.

—J. Oswald Sanders

1

Spiritual Maturity

Let us . . . continue
progressing toward maturity.

HEBREWS 6:1 WILLIAMS N.T.

God has a clearly defined objective for each of His
children—that they might be "conformed to the image
of his Son." He exhorts us to "go on to perfection," or
that spiritual maturity of which Jesus was the perfect
example.

What is the goal of the Christian life? Paul left the
Colossian Christians in no doubt as to his view of
the subject: "We are proclaiming Him . . . in order *to present to God everyone mature through union with Christ*" (Col.
1:28 WILLIAMS N.T.). He set the goal clearly before the
Ephesians: "Until we all attain . . . *to a mature manhood* and
to a perfect measure of Christ's moral stature" (Eph. 4:13
WILLIAMS N.T.).

So then the goal of the Christian life is to attain in

ever-increasing degree the standard of spiritual maturity which was seen in perfection in Christ. John said with keen anticipation: "When we see him, we shall be like him." Could there be any higher glory? In a word, spiritual maturity is Christlikeness. In every life situation our Lord reacted in a mature way. Coleridge was right when he claimed that "beyond that which is found in Jesus Christ, the human race has not and never will progress."

Christ set the standard in everything. He was never petulant, always calm; never rebellious, always obedient; never fearful, always courageous; never vacillating, always resolute; never pessimistic, always cheerful; never subtle, always sincere; never grasping, always generous; never acting from expediency, always from principle. He is the pattern of spiritual maturity.

WHAT IS SPIRITUAL MATURITY?

It is not an automatic process which takes place by mere passage of time. We have to press on to it. Moral earnestness and endeavor are involved if the goal is to be attained.

It is not merely a mental apprehension of spiritual things or the ability to do spiritual work. It is primarily concerned with our attitudes to God and our fellow men. It is the ability to meet the demands and emergencies of everyday life in a mature and not in a childish way. Our Lord commended the childlike spirit but nowhere encouraged a childish attitude in life situations. The spiritually mature Christian is one who is able to function happily in any circumstance. Perhaps a consideration of the marks of *spiritual immaturity* will highlight its opposite. The spiritually immature person meets adult situations and tests with childish and immature reactions. This always produces tension and strain with all the attendant problems. When sorrow strikes, he is inclined to indulge in an orgy of self-centered emotion. If financial reverses occur, he is at a loss to know why this should come to him, and he blames God. When hopes are dashed, he loses heart and drops his bundle. When adversity overtakes him, he is swallowed up in self-pity. In domestic difficulties he indulges in tantrums or sulks and creates an atmosphere that mars home unity. When placed with other difficult people, he falls prey to censorious criticism and "gives as good as he gets." When his will is thwarted by God or man, he becomes rebellious and bitter.

So then our spiritual maturity or immaturity is seen in the manner in which we react to the changing circumstances of life. It should be noted, however, that spiritual maturity does not come to anyone naturally. It has to be learned. Is it not striking that it is recorded of Christ that "though he were a Son, yet learned he obedience by the things which he suffered; and being made perfect, he became the author of eternal salvation" (Heb. 5:8–9)? He alone was fully mature. The rest of us are "going on to maturity." In all of us there are some expressions of our personality in which we react immaturely instead of as mature men of God.

MARKS OF SPIRITUAL MATURITY

Dr. A. W. Tozer has enumerated some of these marks, and we can classify ourselves by bringing our lives alongside this measuring tape. The spiritually mature Christian is characterized by:

A desire to be holy rather than happy. Holiness is attractive only to the mature. A child is far more interested in being happy than in being good. The child has to learn by painful experience that true happiness comes only by way of goodness. Christ was happier than any of His contemporaries because He "loved righteousness, and hated iniquity" (Heb. 1:9).

An attitude of giving rather than receiving. A child prefers receiving to giving. He has to be taught the joy of giving, that sharing is a much happier thing than mere selfish enjoyment. The only authentic saying of our Lord outside those recorded in the Gospels is this: "It is more blessed to give than to receive" (Acts 20:35*b*). He knew this because His was a life of self-giving.

A preference for serving rather than being served. A child enjoys having everyone shower attention on him. Rarely does he think of serving someone else unless he is prompted. Our Lord said: "The Son of man came not to be ministered unto, but to minister" (Mark 10:45).

A joyous personality. The morose and lugubrious person indicates that he is spiritually immature. His very gloom is an evidence of inner conflicts. Christ was so joyous that He was able to bequeath His joy to His disciples.

A fruitful life as opposed to a barren life. The mark of a mature tree is that it reproduces itself. Fruit is the evidence of maturity. Jesus said: "Except a corn of wheat fall into the ground and die, it abideth alone: but if it die, it bringeth forth much fruit" (John 12:24). Only the mature Christian is willing to fall into the ground and die, and only he is spiritually fruitful.

Acceptance rather than evasion of discipline. It is a childish reaction to shun the disciplines of God. While not necessarily enjoying it, the mature Christian does not run away from God's chastening but adapts himself to it. Paul said: "I have learned, in whatsoever state I am, therewith to be content" (Phil. 4:11). He disciplined himself to accept divinely permitted chastening.

A life of love. The highest manifestation of spiritual maturity is love. We are only as mature as we are mature in love. John says that a person who is fear-ridden is immature in love. "There is no fear in love . . . but full-grown (complete, perfect) love turns fear out of doors and expels every trace of terror! . . . he who is afraid has not yet reached the full maturity of love [is not yet grown into love's complete perfection]" (1 John 4:18 AMPC). Christ's perfection was manifested in the fullness of His love.

How do we fare when we bring our lives alongside these tests? Are we making satisfactory progress toward spiritual maturity?

There is another possibility in the Christian life. Spiritual maturity is not maintained automatically. Strange though it may seem, it is possible to degenerate into immaturity again. There is such a thing spiritually as second childhood.

MARKS OF SPIRITUAL DEGENERATION

There is a spiritual equivalent to physical dotage and senility which is not a matter of mere age. It is a solemnizing fact that we can "unknow" truth which we have once appre-hended, and which once gripped and enthralled us. Any Christian who has seriously backslidden is very conscious of this.

The writer of the letter to the Hebrews emphasizes this possibility. "*Ye are become* dull of hearing. When for the time ye ought to be teachers, *ye are become* such as need someone to teach you" (Heb. 5:11–12, lit. trans.). They were not always dull of hearing, the correct tense of the verb suggests. Once they were responsive to the truth, but now they have degenerated into spiritual senility.

The divine diagnosis of those who have thus degenerated indicates three realms in which this is evidenced.

Dullness and sluggishness in hearing the Word of God. They are sluggish in achieving spiritual insight. They have become lazy and unwilling for the discipline necessary if the deeper things of God are to be understood and mas-tered. The writer to the Hebrews was bursting to share glorious and deep spiritual truths with them, but they were preoccupied with elementary truth. "I have much to say to you about Him, but it is difficult to make it clear to you, since you have become so dull in your spiritual senses" (Heb. 5:11 WILLIAMS N.T.).

It is a grand thing to love "the simple gospel," but this can be a mark either of spiritual immaturity or of degener-acy. God forbid that we should ever cease to love *the gospel in its simplicity*, but we must not be content to stay there. We must go on to appreciate increasingly *the gospel in its profundity*. We will rejoice in the truth of the cross as substi-tution, but we must go on to appreciate our identification with Christ on the cross. "So then let us once for all quit the elementary teaching about Christ and continue progressing toward maturity" (Heb. 6:1 WILLIAMS N.T.).

Inability to teach others. The mature Christian is always seizing opportunities of taking in and imparting truth. He is always on the lookout for occasions to teach others and share his own discoveries in the Word, whether he does it formally or informally. These Hebrew Christians had lost that zest to teach and were content to receive all they could for their sluggish, overfed souls. They had become spiritually self-absorbed. Teaching others what we have learned is one of the best ways of stimulating our own appetite for the truth of God.

Reversion to infancy. "You actually need someone to teach you over and over again the very elements of the truths that God has given us, and you have gotten into such a state that you are in constant need of milk instead of solid food" (Heb. 5:12 WILLIAMS). The new convert must of course be indoctrinated with the *ABC* of the gospel. The milk of the Word is the only food appropriate for him. But when a Christian of some years' standing who has known and experienced some of the more advanced teachings of Scripture loses taste for meat and reverts to milk, it is a sign of spiritual degeneracy.

The writer to the Hebrews insists on the necessity of constant progress in the Christian life. There is no such thing as static Christianity. We will not give up any of the elementary teaching about Christ, but we must move on to the next class. "And let us be borne onwards to full maturity; for we cannot be laying the foundations all the time."[1]

The divine prescription is that instead of slipping back, we go on to perfection or full maturity, and this demands deliberate and decisive action. Maturity requires full obedience to the conditions of discipleship laid down by our Master. The terms may seem hard, but they are no harder than He fulfilled Himself. We can count on God doing His part in giving the help of the Holy Spirit, but there is a part for us to do as well. There are four elements in the divine prescription for spiritual maturity.

Get to know Christ as High Priest. This is the whole thrust of chapters four to six of the Hebrews letter. Get to know Him as the One who is able to succor (Heb. 2:17–18), to sympathize (Heb. 4:15), and to save (Heb. 7:25). We know Him as our Savior who brings pardon and peace. That is the *ABC* of the gospel. We must go on to know Him as our High Priest who secures access for us into the very presence of God, who maintains us in constant fellowship with God, who presents our prayers by virtue of His own merits, and ever lives to make intercession for us.

Engage in teaching the truth you know to others (Heb. 5:12). Unused powers tend to atrophy. When Charles Darwin was a young man, he was passionately fond of poetry and music. But he became so fascinated with his scientific studies and research that for many years he had

1. Hebrews 6:1, William Barclay, *The Letter to the Hebrews*, The Daily Study Bible (Edinburgh: The St. Andrew Press, 1955), 50.

no time for his former pursuits. When he retired and once again took up poetry and music, he discovered, to his dismay, that he had lost the taste for them. His powers of appreciation of music and literature had atrophied.

If we pass on what we know by letter or conversation as well as in formal Bible teaching, this will develop both capacity and desire. "To him that hath shall be given" is a spiritual principle of perpetual relevance. The more we teach, the more we will understand.

Exercise your spiritual faculties. "Solid food belongs to full-grown men who on account of constant use have their faculties trained to distinguish good and evil" (Heb. 5:14 WILLIAMS N.T.). We are to engage in spiritual gymnastics if we would reach the goal of spiritual maturity. Prayer, meditation, communion, witness, and study of the Scriptures all develop our spiritual faculties. This is our responsibility.

Count on the enabling of the Holy Spirit. "Let us be borne along to maturity," is the injunction. And who will carry us along? Paul gives the answer: "We all, with open face beholding as in a glass the glory of the Lord, are changed into the same image [of spiritual maturity] from glory to glory, *even as by the Spirit of the Lord*" (2 Cor. 3:18).

2

God's Pattern Servant

Behold my servant.

ISAIAH 42:1

There is only One who has demonstrated to the world
full spiritual maturity, only One in whom the Father
found unqualified delight. The prophet Isaiah, guided
by the Spirit, foretold the winsome characteristics of
God's ideal Servant.

In the prophecy of Isaiah the phrase "servant of the
LORD" is used in three distinct senses. It is used of the
nation of Israel. "But thou, Israel . . . my servant" (41:8).
It is used of the children of God. "This is the heritage of
the servants of the LORD, and their righteousness is of me,
saith the LORD" (54:17). It is used anticipatively of Christ.
"Behold my servant, whom I uphold; mine elect, in whom
my soul delighteth" (42:1).

God selected Israel to represent Him and to be a light

among the godless nations of the world. But the nation failed Him at every turn. His Son, the pattern Servant, rendered a devotion and service which Israel failed to give and met the highest ideal of God and man. His service to God is the pattern of ours. Only twice in Scripture is Christ specifically stated to be our example. Once it is in connection with service and once with suffering.

In the supreme revelation of lowly service recorded in John 13, our Lord specifically stated that He was leaving us an example. Such service was no new office for Him, for He is "the same yesterday, and to day, and for ever" (Heb. 13:8). He was only manifesting in time what He had always been in eternity. On that occasion He acted out the master principle of service—that the highest honor lies in the lowliest service. The life of God is spent in service to humanity. There is no one so perpetually available as He. He rules all because He serves all. Jesus therefore taught and exemplified that he who would be great must become the servant of all.

THE CHARACTER OF GOD'S SERVANT

In Isaiah 42:1–4 the prophet predicts six qualities of character which would mark God's pattern Servant, and which should therefore be seen increasingly in us.

Dependence. "My servant, whom I uphold" (v. 1). This is one of the amazing aspects of the self-emptying of our Lord. In His incarnation, He did not divest Himself of any of His divine attributes or prerogatives. But although He was "upholding all things by the word of his power" (Heb. 1:3), so closely did He identify Himself with us in all the infirmities of our human nature, that He too required divine upholding. Consider these statements:

"The Son can do nothing of himself" (John 5:19).

"The word which ye hear is not mine" (John 14:24).

"My doctrine is not mine" (John 7:16).

"The works which the Father hath given me to finish, the same works . . . I do" (John 5:36).

Taken together these verses clearly indicate that our Lord chose to be dependent on His Father for both His words and His works. Are we as totally dependent on the Father as Jesus was? Surely we need the divine upholding much more than He.

Acceptance. "My servant . . . in whom my soul delighteth" (v. 1). Although God met with little more than disappointment in His servant Israel, He was delighted in Christ. On two occasions He broke the silence of eternity to refer to His Son as the One in whom He was well pleased. He was the Servant who never failed to shed abroad the aroma of a self-forgetful ministry.

Modesty. "He shall not cry, nor lift up, nor cause his voice to be heard in the street" (v. 2). The literal meaning of the words used here is "He shall not be loud or screamy." In His service self-advertisement was entirely absent. He silenced those who would blazon abroad His miracles. The essential elements in the training of a good servant are discipline, self-effacement, and submission, and each of these qualities was evidenced by our Lord. He stole away from the adulation of the crowds. He performed no miracle merely to enhance His own prestige. "God's highest artists do not inscribe their names on the canvas."

Compassion. "A bruised reed shall he not break, and the smoking flax shall he not quench" (v. 3). God's servant will show mercy to the weak and erring. This is the class generally despised or ignored. Jesus specialized in helping such people. There is no life so bruised and broken that He will not save and restore. The superficial Christian worker is inclined to bypass these derelicts in order to devote his powers to others of a higher stratum of society whom he considers more worthy of them. He is not willing to keep on teaching the elements of the gospel to simple believers, adjusting squabbles and endeavoring to win backsliders back to the Lord. Jesus, however, found joy and satisfaction in stooping to serve those whom most ignore. His skillful loving care caused the bruised reed to once again produce heavenly music and fanned the dimly burning wick into a glowing flame.

Peter was surely a bruised reed and a smoldering wick. After his denial the light of his witness was all but extinguished and was powerless to kindle another flame. But the Master personally fanned the spark so effectually that it kindled the Pentecostal conflagration. He granted Peter a special personal interview that saved him for the service of the kingdom.

Optimism. "He shall not fail nor be discouraged, till he have set judgment in the earth" (v. 4). We will search in vain for any pessimism in the life and ministry of the pattern Servant. Jesus evinced an unshakable confidence in the fulfillment of the purposes of the Father and in the coming of the kingdom. His attitude was consistently one of hope and assurance. Hope is an essential element in our battle with the powers of darkness. It is not by accident that the words "fail" and "discouraged" are the same in the

22

original Scriptures as "break" and "quench." The implication is that although Christ engages in His gracious ministry to the bruised reeds and smoking wicks, He himself is neither one nor the other. His optimism will be justified by the achievement of His objective.

Anointing. "Behold my servant . . . I have put my spirit upon him" (v. 1). By themselves, even the foregoing desirable spiritual qualities are insufficient to equip for divine service. It requires the divine enduement of the Spirit to bring them to full effectiveness. "God anointed Jesus of Nazareth with the Holy Ghost and with power: who went about doing good, and healing all that were oppressed of the devil" (Acts 10:38). All that He achieved was by the enabling and empowering of the Holy Spirit.

The Spirit imparts life and power to everything He touches, and the same anointing as Jesus received is open to each of His disciples. We surely should never attempt what our divine Exemplar would not do—embark on our public ministry without being anointed with the Spirit. God does not give the Spirit by measure (John 3:34). It is only our capacity to receive which regulates the supply of the Spirit (Phil. 1:19). It is enough for the servant that he be as his Lord. What happened to Christ at the Jordan and what happened to the church at Pentecost must happen to us if we are ever to fulfill God's ideal for us.

QUALIFICATIONS OF THE HUMAN SERVANT

In his prophecy Isaiah indicates certain qualities and qualifications which are essential to our service for God.

Fire-touched lips. "Lo, this hath touched thy lips" (6:7). Isaiah's ministry began with lips purged by fire from the altar of sacrifice. Before God's servant is qualified to mediate His message, the fountain of his heart and the vehicle of his tongue must first be purged. There must be a burning out of the carnal and a burning in of the spiritual.

Opened ears. "He wakeneth mine ear to hear as the learned" (50:4). And this was an experience which Isaiah enjoyed "morning by morning." His first concern was to listen to the voice of the One who had wakened him in order to obey Him.

Instructed tongue. "The Lord God hath given me the tongue of the learned," or "the tongue of them that are taught" (50:4). The world is full of people who are "weary and heavy-laden." They are weary physically because of the hardness of the way and weary spiritually because of sorrow or perhaps the wages of sin. God's servant required education in the school of suffering, and his education was supervised by none other than God Himself. Even Jesus "learned . . . obedience by the things which he suffered" (Heb. 5:8). He was not exempt from the school of suffering.

In this school the prophet learned to select *the right time* to speak *the right word.* To be effective, his word had to be *in season.* The right word spoken at the wrong time would be like the seed that fell on the wayside. Spoken at the right time, it would fall into prepared soil and become fruitful.

The *manner* in which the word is spoken is as important as the timing and the wording. God taught His servant that he might "know *how* to speak" the healing word. There can be a delicacy and sympathy in presenting even an unpalatable truth which makes it acceptable and therefore doubly effective. A single sentence can save a soul or change a life—"a word in season."

Blinded eyes. "Who is blind, but my servant?" (42:19). The servant of the Lord will be blind to all else but the errand on which he is sent. He will refuse to be distracted or sidetracked. Paul's motto will become his: "This one thing I do" (Phil. 3:13). There are distinct spiritual values in a single-track mind.

Willing feet. "How beautiful upon the mountains are the feet of him that bringeth good tidings" (52:7). The pattern servant will be willing to discharge his commission in the hard places of service. Difficult mountains will not daunt him. Without reluctance or repining he will follow the blood-stained footprints of his Lord.

Mouth like a sharp sword. "He hath made my mouth like a sharp sword" (49:2). God will use the friction of adverse circumstances rightly received to impart a sharp cutting edge to His servant's ministry.

MINISTRIES OF THE HUMAN SERVANT

The believer is called to be both *a minister and a priest.* "Ye shall be named the Priests of the LORD: men shall call you the Ministers of our God" (61:6). The priests ministered to the Lord. The Levites ministered to their brethren. We are privileged to minister to both. We are to offer spiritual sacrifices in the sanctuary and to engage in the manual duties of the house of God as well. We are to keep in balance the worship of God and service to man.

His responsibility is *to mediate the light of the gospel.* He is given as a light to the nations and is privileged to bring light to the spiritually blind. He is entrusted with the task of rescuing the captives from the prison house of sin (42:6–7).

He is *to restore the losses of a church* that has become in part apostate. "Thou shalt be called, The repairer of the breach, The restorer of paths to dwell in" (58:12). There is a place for a constructive contending for the faith. The church has degenerated sadly since Pentecostal days and the servant of the Lord has an important part to play in its revival.

His supreme responsibility and privilege is *to glorify God.* "Thou art my servant . . . in whom I will be glorified" (49:3). In reviewing His earthly life, God's ideal Servant summarized the whole in one sentence: "I have glorified thee on the earth" (John 17:4). The supreme aim of His loyal servants is to achieve the same end. His smile will be the adequate reward for any service, however costly and sacrificial.

If these are our chief concerns, Isaiah assures us we shall experience divine upholding (42:6), the supply of every needed resource (45:2–3), heaven's protection (54:17), and ultimate success (55:11).

3

The Consecrated Life

I beseech you . . . present your bodies
a living sacrifice . . . to God.

ROMANS 12:1

The basic secret of Christ's winsome and holy life of
service to God and man was His complete consecration to the will of His Father. "I delight to do thy will, O
my God" (Ps. 40:8) was His lifelong attitude. In measure as we are similarly consecrated to God, our lives
will be winsome and holy.

It is possible to get to heaven without living a consecrated
life, but the journey there will be barren and disappoint-
ing, since consecration is the doorway to undreamed-of joy.
Neglect it, fail to seek it, and life will be greatly impover-
ished. Welcome it, and life becomes inexpressibly enriched.

POSSIBILITIES OF THE CONSECRATED LIFE

The word "consecration," which occurs infrequently in the Bible, is often used loosely and is confused with "dedication," which is its complement; or with "sanctification," which is its outcome. The root significance of the word is: "separation from a common use and solemn dedication to a sacred use." It combines *separation*, the human responsibility, *dedication*, the human act, and *consecration*, the divine act, God's acceptance of our dedication. When we dedicate our lives to Him, He consecrates us to His service. We dedicate our lives to Him that He may work His will in us. He consecrates us to Himself that He might make us holy.

To Frances Ridley Havergal, author of the church's greatest consecration hymn, the significance of consecration came in a flash. "It was on Advent Sunday," she testified, "that I first saw the blessedness of true consecration. I saw it in a flash, and what you see you can never unsee. There must be full surrender before there can be full blessedness. God admits you by one into the other."

One does not automatically grow into consecration—it is a matter of choice, not of chance. Paul makes this very clear: "I beseech you by the mercies of God that ye *present* your bodies . . .," a definite act of the will.

The consecrated life is *a life dedicated to the will of God*. It has been suggested that in consecration we bring our lives to God as a blank sheet of paper with our names signed at the bottom. Confident of His love, we invite Him to fill in the detail as He will. Having done this, we will,

Paul assures us, "prove what is that good and acceptable
and perfect will of God."

The tense of the word "present" signifies a definite act
that cannot be repeated, though it may be reaffirmed. It
may be helpful to some desirous of making such a transaction with God to use a form of words. Could anything
be more simple and comprehensive than that which the
father of Matthew Henry, the great commentator, taught
his children?

> I take God the Father to be my God;
> I take God the Son to be my Saviour;
> I take the Holy Ghost to be my Sanctifier;
> I take the Word of God to be my rule;
> I take the people of God to be my people;
> And I do hereby dedicate and yield
> my whole self to the Lord;
> And I do this deliberately, freely,
> and forever. Amen.

To thus dedicate the life to the Lord may be costly,
but was not His dedication of Himself to the work of our
redemption infinitely costly? Heathen devotees can often
shame us. A missionary who was watching the construc-
tion of a beautiful temple asked an Indian woman, "How
much will it cost?"

"It is for the gods," she answered. "We do not ask what
it will cost."

Is it possible that we may be holding back our lives from
the living God because of fear of what it might cost?

Dr. Alexander Maclaren said the meaning of being a Christian is that, in response to the gift of a whole Christ, a man gives his whole self to Him.

It is *a life separated to the glory of God.* Inherent in the word "consecration" is the idea of separateness. There must of necessity be separation from sin if there is to be separation to God. "Having therefore these promises . . . let us cleanse ourselves from all filthiness of the flesh and spirit" is Paul's exhortation (2 Cor. 7:1). Here again "cleanse" implies a definite, deliberate act. We can renounce everything we know to be wrong by a resolute act of our renewed wills, reinforced by the Holy Spirit (Phil. 2:12–13).

But the separation envisaged is not the separation of the monastery. It is *insulation* from what is sinful rather than *isolation* from it. We have to go on living in a sinful world and among sinful people. It is not merely a negative thing. The consecrated Christian hates evil, but he has a passion for the right and for the glory of God and Christ. He tests all his actions by the one standard, "Is this for the glory of God?" He will do anything, suffer anything, if only God is glorified. Nothing is too costly to give to the Master. Sacrifice has been described as the ecstasy of giving the best we have to the One we love the most.

Then it is *a life concentrated on the service of God.* Robert Lee tells of a convert who was testifying to the fact that the Lord had helped him along the line of consecration. But he had not gotten the word correctly. He said it two or three times like this: "I'm so glad He helped me to be wholly concentrated unto Him." He may have used the wrong word but he expressed the right idea.

Consecration will always issue in concentration on God and His service. It is not an end in itself. If it does not find expression in holy activity, it is spurious. Like Paul, the consecrated Christian can say, "This one thing I do." Realizing that he is to be the medium of conveying the words of eternal life to a world astray from God, he devotes himself without reserve to that sacred task.

Some years ago, King George VI of England was broadcasting to the world from the U.S.A. Someone tripped over the wires in the studio of CBS and, for a moment, the king's message went off the air. Harold Vivian, the radio engineer, taking in the situation, literally spliced the broken link with his body, and made it possible for the king's message to come through. He grasped the wires with his hands and held on for twenty minutes until new wires could be connected. He literally presented his body a living sacrifice that the king's message might reach the world. Shall we not similarly consecrate ourselves body, soul, and spirit to God, that through us the only message of hope may reach the world of lost men?

PERILS OF THE CONSECRATED LIFE

Though there are glorious possibilities in this life, there are also very real perils and pitfalls. But is this not only to be expected? If there is a devil who is implacably hostile to God, is it surprising if he endeavors to lure us away from Him? It is for us to be prepared for his assaults and to depend on the Christ who dwells within to make us more than conquerors.

There is *the peril of laxity*. With the crisis of consecration passed, it may be thought that one could safely relax a little, that there would not be the same need to be punctilious in nurturing the inner life. Some have thought that the joy and flow of new spiritual life which may have accompanied their surrender would ensure continued spiritual progress without so much prayer and Bible study. On the contrary, never were these more essential. As a child grows, it requires more food, not less. And as one's spiritual capacity increases, the strong meat of the Word becomes more necessary to maintain robust health. A fire cannot be maintained without constant stoking. The fuel is the Word of God.

Nor is there any substitute for prayer—communion with God and unselfish intercession for others. This is the only atmosphere in which the consecrated life can be maintained. These devotional exercises are not an end in themselves, but through them we maintain uninterrupted vital union with Christ. We must beware of laxity.

There is *the peril of presumption*. A newly won victory over sin has deceived some into thinking that sin itself had been annihilated and eradicated. Presuming that sin had been plucked out of their hearts, they became unwatchful and negligent. When sin reappeared in their lives they were faced with two alternatives: either to call these sins infirmities, or to deny the reality of their experience of consecration and go back to the old life of defeat. In either case they forfeited the true joy of consecration and grieved the Holy Spirit.

We must guard against holding low views of sin. The demands of God's holiness are not on a sliding scale to meet our need and infirmities. Nowhere in Scripture is it either asserted or implied that the principle of sin has been eradicated, nor is there a single example of it recorded. John expressly warned against such an assumption: "If we say that we have no sin, we deceive ourselves, and the truth is not in us" (1 John 1:8).

Even in the consecrated Christian it is tragically possible for the self life and the sins of the flesh to reassert themselves. It is essential that we "walk in the Spirit" if we are not to fulfill the lusts of the flesh (Gal. 5:16). Let us beware of presuming that sin is eradicated.

There is *the peril of superiority*. Full consecration usually brings with it such a vital experience and spiritual illumination that there can be the tendency to be critical of others who may not appear to share the same exuberance or manifest the same outward zeal. Some, in the flush of their newfound joy, have returned from conferences and conventions to criticize ministers and fellow Christians rather than to walk humbly with God. Spiritual pride is the root of such an attitude which merits the censure of Isaiah 65:5–6: "A people . . . which say, Stand by thyself, come not near to me; for I am holier than thou. These are a smoke in my nose, a fire that burneth all the day . . . I will . . . recompense, even recompense into their bosom." Any experience we enjoy is the gift of God and affords no occasion for vaunting ourselves. We must beware of censoriousness or superiority.

There is *the peril of self-confidence*. In ourselves, we are no stronger after consecration than before. Our strength is derived from Christ to whom we are now rightly related.

We are strong only so long as we maintain contact with Him. Immediately after Israel's glorious triumph at Jericho, the key city of Canaan, they were put to flight by little Ai. They were so sure of themselves that they felt no need to consult their Commander. Had they not defeated Jericho? They paid dearly for their self-confidence. Not until they dealt with their sin and rendered implicit obedience did victory return. Our strength lies in self-distrust rather than self-confidence.

There is *the peril of the emotions*. Frequently, emotions are deeply stirred at the crisis of consecration, with the result that joyous feelings are thought to be the essence of the experience. This is not so. The joyous feelings are only incidental to the transaction, which can be just as real without them. The degree of emotional response is largely a matter of temperament. Continuous thrills are not necessary, nor are they often given. A subsiding of the emotions does not in any way affect the reality of the unchanging facts which form the basis of true Christian experience. We must learn to live in the region of the will, not in the changeful realm of the feelings. It is what we *choose*, not what we *feel*, that is important. God wants us to trust Himself and not supernatural experiences or stirred emotions. We must beware of undue emphasis on feelings.

The consecrated life is one of true sanity—it is "our reasonable, our logical service." Dr. A. S. Way translates this clause thus: "The necessity of this rite of consecration follows from all the argument." It is the logical issue of the acceptance of the blessings which flow from our union with Christ. It is reasonable because God uses human instrumentality and needs us in His purpose of blessing for mankind. It is reasonable in view of what we owe to God for what He has bestowed on us.

> All for Jesus! all for Jesus!
>> All my being's ransomed powers;
> All my thoughts and words and doings,
>> All my days and all my hours.
> Let my hands perform His bidding;
>> Let my feet run in His ways;
> Let mine eyes see Jesus only;
>> Let my lips speak forth His praise.
> —MARY DAGWORTHY JAMES (1810–1883)

4

Bringing Back the King

Why speak ye not a word
of bringing the king back?

2 SAMUEL 19:10

The consecrated life is often ushered in by a crisis of
surrender to the lordship of Christ. Where His sovereignty is gladly welcomed and accepted, the Holy
Spirit is able to reproduce Christ's holy life in that of
the believer.

O f all the notable men of the Old Testament, none has
so fully bared his heart as King David. His psalms are
often autobiographical, and reflect the heights of elation
and depths of desolation which formed part of his experience. But there is no story more poignant than his flight
from the throne before Absalom, his favorite son (2 Sam.
15). From this moving episode and its sequel we can draw
lessons which relate to great David's Greater Son.

THE CAUSE OF THE KING'S ABSENCE

David was growing old and his reign had lost the vivid color which had marked its earlier years, when he and his men had been almost idolized by the people. The glamour of former victories had been forgotten. The conquest of the invincible Goliath with sling and stone was but a tale often told. The aging king was unable to devote the same time and attention to hearing the grievances of the people. The memory of the public is notoriously short. One day they will laud Winston Churchill as the savior of the nation. Next day they will vote him out of office. One day they will cry, "All hail!" to Jesus. The next, their cry will be, "Crucify Him!"

The very people who had worshiped David were now disgruntled, and his unworthy son Absalom was not slow to exploit his father's waning popularity. Absalom, like David's other sons, had seldom been thwarted by his father and had grown proud and headstrong. All the circumstances were favorable to his plot to usurp his father's throne.

Like many politicians of later days, the handsome Absalom promised the people a more liberal government. Sitting in the gate, he ingratiated himself with the people with extravagant promises. "Oh that I were made judge in the land, that every man which hath any suit or cause might come unto me, and I would do him justice!" (2 Sam. 15:4). So Absalom stole the hearts of the men of Israel. He had a keen eye for pageantry and publicity, and his handsome equipage contrasted more than favorably with the simplicity of David in his declining years.

Four years of constant subversion fostered by Absalom and his friends so undermined David's throne that the people rebelled, and David was driven into exile. However, he rallied his loyal forces and decisively defeated and routed Absalom and his followers. In the course of battle, and contrary to David's instructions, Absalom was killed.

This totally unexpected turn of events threw the nation into confusion. They were thoroughly disillusioned. Absalom had promised so much and performed so little. The old king who had been their deliverer on so many occasions was in ignominious exile, and the new king was dead. Their hearts smote them for their ingratitude, and once again their thoughts turned to their old hero. With the renewal of allegiance came the rekindling of love, and they were soon vying for the honor of bringing the king back. "The king saved us out of the hand of our enemies, and he delivered us out of the hand of the Philistines; . . . And Absalom, whom we anointed over us, is dead in battle. Now therefore why speak ye not a word of bringing the king back?" (2 Sam. 19:9–10).

There is a striking parallel between David and Christ. Our Lord too has His rightful kingdom, none the less real because spiritual. The great salvation texts which we associate with His saviorhood are linked also with His sovereignty. For example: "If thou shalt confess with thy mouth *Jesus as Lord*, and shalt believe in thy heart that God hath raised him from the dead, thou shalt be saved" (Rom. 10:9 ASV). Saving faith is commitment to Christ as a whole person. Faith cannot choose to be committed to Him in the role of Savior and not in the role of Sovereign Lord.

"God hath made that same Jesus . . . *both Lord and Christ*" (Acts 2:36). "Him hath God exalted . . . to be *a Prince and a Saviour*" (Acts 5:31). We cannot divorce His saviorhood from His sovereignty. How can we accept the immediate purpose of Christ's death, forgiveness, and reject its ultimate purpose, holiness?

In too many lives the rebellion of Absalom has been reenacted, and to all intents and purposes Christ is in exile, driven practically from His throne by the very people He had delivered by His cross. When Garibaldi had delivered Italy from her aggressors at great personal sacrifice and suffering, he was hailed as the savior of the nation. No flattery too fulsome, no praises too extreme for the national hero. One grateful group in the nation contended that the logical recognition for his service would be to place him on the throne. His saviorhood entitled him to sovereignty. Others, though glad enough to enjoy the blessings which accrued from his bravery, disputed his right to sovereignty. They desired to retain power in their own hands. For a few days he was actually put in prison by those whom he had saved from the invading hordes. He was later banished to the island of Capri.

The crucial question for us all: "Is Christ on the throne of my life as undisputed king, or has He to all intents and purposes been forced into unwilling exile?" Do we unquestioningly take our orders from Him? Because He is Savior, we take from Him the gifts He offers. Because He is Sovereign, we give back to Him our whole lives in loyal service.

It is to be noted that David did not voluntarily leave his throne for exile. The people forsook him, he did not forsake them. The usurper stole their hearts and they placed him on the throne, thus ousting the rightful occupant. Satan knows how to steal hearts and alienate them from Christ. He knows how to exploit the weak points of our characters, even as Absalom made Israel feel they were losing something by being loyal to David, and their interests would be better served by him. The enemy adopts the same tactics today. "Whenever any object, lawful or unlawful, is loved and served more than Jesus Christ, the rebellion of Absalom is repeated."

CRITERIA OF THE KING'S ABSENCE

It is customary when a king is in residence that his flag flies over his palace. The flag is the outward symbol indicating that he is present and exercising his sovereignty. From the experience of David and his people in this episode, we can draw a parallel with the Christian in whose life Christ is not at the moment Reigning Monarch. There will be certain unmistakable criteria:

A Sense of Dissatisfaction (2 Sam. 19:9). The people recalled with acute nostalgia the days of David's glory, and now that he was in exile, the throne was empty and all seemed stale, flat, and unprofitable. When Christ is not on the throne of a life, prayer becomes unattractive, the Bible dull, and fellowship with Christ only a wistful memory. William Cowper's lament becomes appropriate:

> Where is the blessedness I knew
> When first I saw the Lord?

Where is the soul-refreshing view
Of Jesus and His Word?

It was dissatisfaction and disillusionment that drove the people to bring David back, and to reaffirm his kingship. It is our loving Lord who induces dissatisfaction and produces disillusionment because He loves us too dearly to allow us to remain content in rebellion against Him.

Disregard of the King's Honor. In former days they had counted it an honor to serve David. For his sake they had been prepared to sacrifice their own comforts and interests. To some of them a breathed wish had all the force of an express command. His mighty men had hazarded their lives to gratify his desire for a drink from the well of Bethlehem (2 Sam. 23:15).

But after Absalom's intrigue all was different. Love for David had waned and allegiance had been transferred to the usurper. Is there a like condition with us? Does the Lord say of us as of the Ephesian Christians: "I have this against you, that you no longer love me as you did at the first"? Can He remember days when our love was more warm and sacrificial? Unexpected difficulties met on life's pathway may have discouraged us. The exaltation of King Jesus is no longer the inspiring motive of our love and service.

Indifference to the King's Favor. In former days Israel had delighted in the favor of King David. Now they had allowed him to be driven into exile and cursed by his enemies. Can we remember days when it was sheer delight to spend an hour in the presence of the King, when His favor meant life to us? In those days distance was intolerable, for that is something love cannot endure. Have we grown used to long intervals of estrangement during which we have no vital intercourse with the King?

Queen Victoria of England was a firm believer in the return of Christ as King. On one occasion she said to Dean Farrar: "Oh, how I wish the Lord would come during my lifetime!" "And why, your Majesty?" he asked. "Because I should love to lay my crown at His feet." To her Christ was not only Savior but Sovereign.

CONDITIONS OF THE KING'S RETURN

David longed to return to his throne, but in spite of his desire he was not prepared to return unconditionally. It was not sufficient that his people should regret their disloyalty and defection. Before he would return and again assume the prerogatives of his throne, certain things would have to be put right, and these matters have their counterpart in our relationship with Christ. The three essential conditions for the king's return to reign were:

An Undivided Kingdom. Jealousy and division had separated Judah and Israel and, to David's dismay, it was Israel which had been first to speak of bringing him back. Judah, his first love, had made no move to secure his return. His plea to them was most poignant: "Ye are my brethren, ye are my bones and my flesh: wherefore then are ye the last to bring back the king?" (2 Sam. 19:12).

Christ has the same rights of kinship and kingship. He is bone of our bone and flesh of our flesh. He must see an end to civil war in the soul. He will not consent to rule over a divided kingdom.

A Unanimous Request. David refused to force himself on a reluctant people. He used every legitimate means to induce them to invite him back, but not until they sent an urgent request did he make a move. "And he bowed the heart of all the men of Judah, even as the heart of one man; so that they sent this word unto the king, Return thou, and all thy servants. So the king returned" (2 Sam. 19:14–15). It was gracious of the rejected king to respond so readily after such base ingratitude. And how like his Greater Son!

An Uncompromising Allegiance. Before the kingdom could again be established, the leader of the rebellion, Sheba, had to be punished. The traitor must be dealt with. The king must command the fullest allegiance of his subjects and crush all rebellion.

Before Christ consents to reassume the throne of the kingdom of Mansoul, He may have to do something drastic in our lives to terminate our rebellion. If we will not deal with things that are wrong ourselves, He may have to take the initiative. "If thy right eye offend thee, pluck it out, and cast it from thee: for it is profitable for thee that one of thy members should perish, and not that thy whole body should be cast into hell" (Matt. 5:29). This indicates that we must deal drastically with our sin, for if we do not, God will do so.

David did not assume the throne automatically. The people had something to do, and until they did it he would not move. There had to be the glad consent of the people and the definite invitation to take the throne.

Do you feel the need of someone to control and unify your life? Christ is utterly worthy and completely competent to be king of your life. Abner spoke words which fittingly climax this chapter: "Ye sought for David in times past to be king over you: now then do it" (2 Sam. 3:17–18). Use that regal faculty with which you have been endowed, your will. Renounce all other allegiances. Invite Him to ascend the throne of your heart. Now then do it.

> King of my life, I crown Thee now,
>   Thine shall the glory be,
> Lest I forget Thy thorn-crowned brow,
>   Lead me to Calvary.
> —Jennie Evelyn Hussey (1874–1958)

5

Out of Touch with God

He [Samson] wist not that
the LORD was departed from him.

JUDGES 16:20

The Spirit of the LORD departed from Saul.

1 SAMUEL 16:14

It is possible to have once lived a life of consecration to
God and then, by deliberate sin or by simple neglect,
to get out of touch with God. This affects not only ourselves but those whom we could have influenced for
God had we been in touch with Him.

O ne of the distinctive characteristics of human love is
its hatred of distance. Once nearness has been experienced, distance becomes intolerable. Love knows no suffering more poignant than that of being out of touch with
the lover. If this is true of man's love for man, it is no less
true of love to God, for once the child of God has experienced the transcendent joy of fellowship with Him, he can

never be at rest while that relationship is broken. Yet, is it wrong to suggest that there are multitudes of Christians who have grown almost accustomed to being out of touch with God? Although it is not without regret that they recall the blessedness they knew when they first saw the Lord, yet they have come to regard living at a distance from Him as almost inevitable.

But lost fellowship with God *can* be restored. The way back is not easy or costless, but it is possible. The loss of a limb or the loss of an eye is trivial in comparison with loss of divine fellowship, because our relationship with God affects not only this life but the life which is to come; not only our own lives but the lives of all with whom we come into contact.

May I ask the reader if he is really in touch with God, if he is basking in the light of His countenance and enjoying the sunshine of His smile? We must not just take it for granted that we are in touch with God. Joseph and Mary lost a whole day of fellowship with Jesus because they "supposed him to be in the company." They took for granted something of which they should have made sure.

"He [Samson] wist not that the LORD was departed from him" (Judg. 16:20). He was out of touch with God and did not know it. That was the tragedy of his life. It is very possible for our past experience of Christ to be much brighter than our present enjoyment. This was true of God's espoused people to whom He addressed these plaintive words: "I remember thee, the kindness of thy youth, the love of thine espousals, when thou wentest after me in the wilderness, in a land that was not sown" (Jer. 2:2). God recalled with sad joy the spontaneous glow and warmth of the early love of His people perhaps as He recalls our early love for Him—love that was selfless and sacrificial, love that did not count the cost. When we are out of touch with God, the element of sacrifice disappears, and we serve God only insofar as it does not conflict with our comforts and desires. God remembers and challenges us: "Thou hast left thy first love. Remember therefore from whence thou art fallen, and repent" (Rev. 2:4–5).

A GLORIOUS REALITY

Perhaps some who read these pages seriously question the possibility of living a life constantly in touch with God. Scripture, however, seems to encourage this expectation, for even at the dawn of history Enoch walked with God for three hundred years and when he was translated, "he had this testimony, that he pleased God" (Heb. 11:5). He had none of the aids to devotion which are available to us today—not even a Bible—and yet he walked in daily touch with God. The New Testament abounds in passages which hold out the prospect of triumph in Christ, and these expectations have been realized in countless lives.

Charles Haddon Spurgeon affirmed that in many years he had not known more than a quarter of an hour out of fellowship with God. When Mrs. J. Hudson Taylor was nearing the pearly gates, she turned to her husband and said: "You know, my dear, that for the past ten years there has been no cloud between my Lord and me." That certainly sounds as though such a life is possible.

Frances Ridley Havergal, the much-loved hymn writer,

was the victim of a besetting sin which, in spite of prayers and tears, constantly caused her to lose touch with God. Time and again she came to God with contrite heart asking forgiveness and seeking restoration, only to fail as before. One day, when almost in despair, a verse of Scripture came to her with the authority of God: "The Egyptians whom ye have seen to day, ye shall see them again no more for ever" (Ex. 14:13). "What, Lord, no more forever?" was her amazed response. It was as though a voice replied, "No more forever." She believed God, and rose from her knees, so her sister records, never again to fall before that besetting sin. From that time her poems took on a new tone and character.

> I never thought it could be thus,
>   Month after month to know
> The river of thy peace without
>   One ripple in its flow,
> Without one quiver in the trust,
>   One flicker in its glow.

Or again:

> Like a river glorious
>   Is God's perfect peace,
> Over all victorious
>   In its bright increase.
> Perfect, yet it floweth
>   Fuller every day,
> Perfect, yet it groweth
>   Deeper all the way.

Such a life is not a wistful mirage but a glorious reality.

A TRAGIC POSSIBILITY

Two Old Testament characters illustrate another possibility. The first is Saul, the king who got out of touch with God *deliberately through disobedience.* The second is Samson, who got out of touch with God *unconsciously through presumption.*

No life began with fairer prospects than that of Saul. Physically he was handsome and yet he was modest. When he was anointed king of Israel, God gave him another heart. The Spirit of God came upon him and he prophesied. But before long, as we all inevitably must, Saul found himself traversing "the measured mile." All unknown to him he was entering upon a test which would determine the future of his kingdom. He was charged by God to destroy the crafty and ruthless Amalekites, the enemies of Israel and God. His instructions were crystal clear: "Smite . . . utterly destroy . . . spare . . . not" (1 Sam. 15:3). In the ensuing battle, God granted Saul a resounding victory, but he disobediently spared the best of the sheep and oxen while destroying the diseased and worthless. He also spared Agag the king.

Before we condemn Saul too harshly, let us assure ourselves that we have not been guilty of similar disobedience. We may be glad enough to be rid of disgraceful and degrading sins that hurt our self-esteem, but have we spared well-loved sins, favorite indulgences, or habits about which the Spirit of God has spoken to us time and again? In condemning Saul, we may be condemning ourselves.

When Samuel appeared, Saul shrank from his piercing eye and met him with the pious but uneasy greeting: "I have performed the commandment of the LORD" (1 Sam. 15:13). Samuel's reply was a disconcerting question: "What meaneth then this bleating of the sheep . . . and the lowing of the oxen which I hear? [Dead sheep don't bleat, Saul.] Wherefore then didst thou not obey the voice of the LORD? . . . to obey is better than sacrifice, and to hearken than the fat of rams" (1 Sam. 15:14, 19, 22).

Saul could stifle his conscience, but he could not muffle the bleating of the sheep he should have killed. Nor can we! Are our hearts vocal? Does God's ear detect the bleating of some unconfessed sin, some unforgiven injury, some unpaid debt, or some unrestored property? Does He hear the lowing of some bestial passion which has us in its grip? We may have grown so used to the bleating and lowing that we hardly notice it now, but others can detect it, and God hears it.

Saul saved a flock but lost a kingdom. "When Saul enquired of the LORD," the record runs, "the LORD answered him not" (1 Sam. 28:6). "The Spirit of the LORD departed from Saul" (1 Sam. 16:14). He was deliberately out of touch through disobedience. He died at last at the hand of an Amalekite whom he had spared. If we spare our sins, like Saul we will forfeit our crown.

Samson lost touch with God *unconsciously through presumption*. His, too, was a life bright with promise. When he reached maturity, he had ratified the vow of entire consecration which his parents had taken for him in his infancy. On him, too, the Spirit had descended and through His power Samson achieved mighty exploits against Israel's enemies. His strength lay not in gigantic stature, nor in bulging muscles, but in the power of the Spirit. Once that power was withdrawn, once contact with God was broken, he became, as he said, "like any other man."

So accustomed did Samson become to the cooperation of the Spirit, that he grew presumptuous and trifled with the secret of his strength. He had repeatedly broken his consecration vow, but God in grace continued to empower him for his conflict with the Philistines. To all appearances he was still in touch with God.

After many attempts, the perfidious Delilah wrested Samson's secret from him, put him to sleep on her knees, and caused the locks of his consecration to be cut off. At the familiar cry, "The Philistines be upon thee, Samson," he awoke from his sleep and said, "I will go out as at other times before, and shake myself." And we read in the Scripture, *"He wist not that the LORD was departed from him"* (Judg. 16:20). He was unconsciously out of touch with God! His eyes were put out, and the champion of Israel became the clown of the Philistines. What a tragic end to a promising life because he presumed on the goodness of God while continuing in disobedience.

We must beware of presuming that because we have been in touch with God in the past or because His blessing has rested on our service, therefore all is right now.

Perhaps the most serious aspect of being out of touch with God is that none of us lives unto himself. All the time we live, our lives are making an impact on other lives. There is a startling verse in Numbers 19:22: "And whatsoever

CULTIVATION OF CHRISTIAN CHARACTER

the unclean person toucheth shall be unclean." Out of touch with God, we cannot help but influence others in an unspiritual way. Our works become "dead works," and we become a savor of death instead of a savor of life. One of the solemn revelations of the Judgment Day will be the revelation of the effect of our unconscious influence, the unveiling of what we might have been and achieved had we walked in unbroken fellowship with God; the souls we might have won, the money we might have given, and the burdens we might have lifted.

> Only a smile, yes, only a smile
> That a woman o'erburdened with grief
> Expected from you. 'Twould have given her relief,
> For her heart ached sore the while;
> But weary and cheerless she went away,
> Because, as it happened, that very day
> You were "out of touch" with your Lord.

> Only a word, yes, only a word
> That the Spirit's small voice whispered "speak";
> But the workers passed onward unblessed and weak,
> Whom you were meant to have stirred
> To courage, devotion and love anew,
> Because when the message came to you,
> You were "out of touch" with your Lord.

> Only a note, yes, only a note
> To a friend in a distant land.
> The Spirit said "Write," but then you had planned

Some different work, and you thought
It mattered little. You did not know
'Twould have saved a soul from sin and woe;
    You were "out of touch" with your Lord.

Only a song, yes, only a song
That the Spirit said, "Sing to-night,
Thy voice is thy Master's by purchased right;"
    But you thought, " 'Mid this motley throng,
I care not to sing of the city of gold"—
And the heart your words might have reached grew cold,
    You were "out of touch" with your Lord.

Only a day, yes, only a day!
But oh, can you guess, my friend,
Where the influence reaches, and where it will end,
    Of the hours that you frittered away?
The Master's command is, "Abide in Me,"
And fruitless and vain will your service be
    If "out of touch" with your Lord.
    —JEAN H. WATSON

6

The Spirit-Controlled Life

Be not drunk with wine . . .
be filled with the Spirit.

EPHESIANS 5:18

There is no need for anyone to remain out of touch
with God. He delights to restore and recommission
any who are willing to confess their sin and failure and
place their lives under the control of His Spirit.

If the reader was asked, "Do you know the Holy Spirit?"
the answer would doubtless be in the affirmative. But do
we know the Holy Spirit in the same sense as we know the
Father in His pitying care and paternal chastening, or the
Lord Jesus in His relationship as our Savior and Friend?
We should be able to say with equal assurance of the Holy
Spirit, "I know Him." There is a great difference between
knowing a person and knowing about him. I know about
the President of the United States, but I do not know him.
In John 14:7 our Lord said: "If ye had known me, ye

should have known my Father also." In verse 17 He spoke of "the Spirit of truth; whom the world cannot receive, because it seeth him not, neither knoweth him: *but ye know him.*" The lesson is clear. The Holy Spirit is not an influence or force but a real, living Person whom we can know in the same way as we know the Father and the Son and with whom we can have fellowship. We can know Him as Comforter, Fortifier, Sanctifier. Such knowledge is absolutely essential to a satisfying Christian experience and fruitful service.

It is possible for us to thoughtlessly ignore the Holy Spirit. We would not do it willfully, but the practical effect is the same. We should recognize Him day by day, remembering that He is of equal power and of equal glory with the Father and the Son. He is worthy of equal worship and reverence and love, for He is God.

"BE FILLED WITH THE SPIRIT"

What does this apostolic injunction in Ephesians 5:18 mean? It is not an invitation to realize a privilege but a command to fulfill an obligation. There is probably no more frequent prayer petition than: "Lord, fill me with Thy Holy Spirit." Yet there seldom appears to be equal assurance that the prayer has been answered. What do we expect to happen when we offer that prayer? Is it something mystical and mysterious? The clear teaching of Scripture is that we are filled with the Spirit when our human spirit is mastered and controlled by the Holy Spirit. The idea behind the command "Be filled with the Spirit" is not so much that of an empty vessel passively waiting for something to be poured into it, as water into a glass. It is rather the concept of a human personality voluntarily surrendered to the domination of the Holy Spirit.

If we look at the manner in which "filled" is used on other occasions, we will get light on this point. "They . . . were filled with fear" (Luke 5:26). When the Lord was breaking the news to His disciples that He was going to leave them, He said: "Because I have said these things unto you, sorrow hath filled your heart" (John 16:6). What does it mean to have hearts filled with fear or sorrow? Thayer says in his lexicon, "That which wholly takes possession of the mind is said to fill it." To have hearts filled with fear or sorrow means that these emotions so take hold of and possess and control heart and mind that other things become of only secondary importance. To be filled with the Spirit, then, means to be controlled by the Spirit.

Perhaps the imperfect illustration of hypnotism may be of some help here. A hypnotized person speaks and acts at the behest of another person to whom he has yielded control of his will. In hypnotism, the subject is passive and allows his mind to go blank, giving himself up to the hypnotist—a very dangerous attitude. But in being filled with the Spirit there is no passivity. Every faculty and power of the Spirit-filled person are constantly in the fullest exercise. The Spirit's control is not automatic but voluntarily and constantly conceded. If the surrender of the personality to the Spirit is withdrawn, His control is thereby broken and His power short-circuited.

The indwelling Holy Spirit will exercise this control

from the center of the yielded believer's personality. He will enlighten the *intellect* so that ever-deepening spiritual truth can be apprehended. As the Spirit of truth, He leads into all truth. He will purify the *affections* and fix them on Christ, for His ministry is always Christocentric. He will reinforce the *will*, weakened by sinful indulgence, and empower to do the will of God. Thus from the very inner citadel of the heart He carries on His gracious ministry.

The fullness of the Spirit does not obliterate personality, as does hypnotism. In fact, the person who is filled with the Spirit only then realizes and discovers his true personality. It is not obliterated but released. We will never know the possibilities of our redeemed personality until we definitely yield ourselves in full and unreserved surrender to His control.

ARE YOU FILLED WITH THE SPIRIT?

This is a question to which a definite answer can and should be given. But how can we know? What is the evidence? The answer is found in the context of the command. A great deal too much emphasis has been laid on the emotional aspect of this experience and far too little on its ethical implications. Our feelings are not the evidence of the Spirit's fullness. The test is—What is the quality of our character and service in the varying relationships of life?

It will be noticed that Ephesians 5:18–21 constitutes a single unbroken sentence. In this paragraph Paul indicates certain characteristics of the Spirit-filled believer. His life will be one of spontaneous praise—"Speaking to yourselves in psalms and hymns and spiritual songs, singing and making melody in your heart to the Lord." He will be a man who is perennially thankful—giving thanks "always *for all things*"—the bad as well as the good. He will be submissive, not self-assertive—"Submitting yourselves one to another." This submission will be mutual, not one-sided, a gracious yieldedness of one to the other. Do we evidence these marks of being Spirit-filled?

The control of the life by the Holy Spirit will have tangible results in *domestic relationships*. Because the Christian home is the citadel of Christianity, the Apostle, guided by the Spirit, shows how Spirit-filled believers will deport themselves in the exacting relationships of homelife. He first addresses *wives*: "Wives, submit yourselves unto your own husbands, as unto the Lord. . . . as the church is subject unto Christ, so let the wives be to their own husbands in every thing" (vv. 22, 24). There is no suggestion here that the wife is inferior to the husband in any sense. It is not a question of the superiority of the husband or the inferiority of the wife, but of the respective positions God in His wisdom has assigned to each. "The husband *is* the head of the wife, even as Christ *is* the head of the church." As it is no dishonor to the church to be subject to Christ, it is no dishonor for the wife to be subject to her husband. Within the marriage relationship, the wife can wield a tremendous influence, but that influence will be greatly enhanced when her divinely ordained position is recognized.

Read by itself, the injunction to wives would seem to be sweeping and unfair, but taken in its context, and read in conjunction with the equally stringent exhortations to *husbands*, it is not so unreasonable as it may at first seem. If all husbands fulfilled the pattern given in verses 25, 28, and 33, wives would find no problem in being subject to them. The Holy Spirit knew that if wives were in danger of failing in subjection to their husbands, there was an equal danger that husbands would not love their wives unselfishly.

"Husbands, love your wives, even as Christ also loved the church, and gave himself for it. . . . So ought men to love their wives as their own bodies. . . . so love his wife even as himself" (vv. 25, 28, 33). The unique element in Christ's love for the church is His utter selflessness, His sacrificial love, and this quality will be seen in ever-increasing measure in the Spirit-filled husband. Love always expresses itself in loving considerateness. The wife has the right to expect from her husband a love that is sacrificial and unselfish. He is to love her as much as he loves himself. Was Paul smiling when he penned the words: "For no man ever yet hated his own flesh; but nourisheth and cherisheth it" (v. 29)?

And what of the *young people* in the family? How will the control of the Spirit in the life express itself? In respectful and loving obedience. "Children, obey your parents in the Lord: for this is right. Honor thy father and mother; which is the first commandment with promise" (6:1–2). This obedience will, of course, be given only to those commands which are not contrary to the Word of God. When parental commands transgress the divine injunctions, we must obey God rather than men. In these days of widespread juvenile delinquency, this apostolic exhortation was never more appropriate, and the indwelling Spirit will enable young people to obey it. The evidence of their being filled with the Spirit will lie not in a thrilling emotional experience but in their honoring and obeying their parents.

The Apostle was sympathetic toward the special problems of youth, so he urged *fathers* not to provoke their children to wrath (6:4). They are not to make it hard for them to obey or to impose unnecessary restrictions. He further enjoins the Spirit-filled father to bring up his children "in the nurture and admonition of the Lord." He will have a family altar in the home where they can learn the ways of the Lord.

Then, too, *business relationships* will feel the impact of the Spirit's control of lives. The relationships between *masters and servants* will be sweetened. Servants will be obedient and serve "in singleness of . . . heart, as unto Christ; not with eyeservice, as menpleasers; but as the servants of Christ, doing the will of God from the heart" (6:5–6). This paragraph reads strangely in the context of today's industrial disputes! Masters are to be considerate and treat their employees as they expect to be treated by them. Paul reminds masters that they too have a Master in heaven to whom they are finally accountable for their service. There is no provision made for slothful or unwilling servants or for parsimonious and oppressive masters. Between Spirit-filled masters and servants no major point of contention could arise.

Do our business relationships bear the marks of the Spirit's control?

In addition to these marks of the Spirit's fullness, there will be other easily discernible features which have been summarized by Miss Ruth Paxson:

The realization of Christ's abiding presence (Eph. 3:17). Since He is the Spirit of Christ, the indwelling Spirit will make Christ the home of our thoughts and affections.

The reproduction of Christ's holy life (Gal. 5:22–23). Since He is the Spirit of holiness, His presence will be manifested in the production of the nine graces which perfectly picture the character of our Lord.

The reenactment of Christ's supernatural power (Acts 1:8). Since He is the Spirit of power, He will impart spiritual power to the one in whom He dwells—power to suffer and sacrifice as well as to work and witness.

7

In Christ—Christ in Us

Of him are ye in Christ Jesus.

1 CORINTHIANS 1:30

Know ye not . . . that Jesus Christ is in you?

2 CORINTHIANS 13:5

When the Holy Spirit is granted control of a life, He delights to guide the believer into the deeper truths of the Word of God. Three basic spiritual truths are: We are in Christ; Christ is in us; Christ is being formed in us.

One of the most blessed functions of the Holy Spirit is to reveal to us the things of Christ. "He shall glorify me," Jesus said, "for he shall receive of mine, and shall shew it unto you" (John 16:14). One of the clearest evidences of the Spirit's control of our lives is not that we are always thinking of Him, but that our thoughts are ever turning to Christ. The Spirit makes us conscious of Christ, not of Himself, for there is no rivalry within the unity of the

Godhead. His ministry is always Christ-centered.

Three things are true of every child of God: (1) He is in Christ. (2) Christ is in him. (3) Christ is to be formed in him.

WE ARE IN CHRIST

"But of him are ye in Christ Jesus, who of God is made unto us wisdom, and righteousness, and sanctification, and redemption" (1 Cor. 1:30). This is not something we have done, but something *God* has done. "Of him," for it is the Father's doing, "are ye"—in spite of weakness and unworthiness—"*in Christ Jesus.*" These three words occupy a very important place in New Testament teaching. In fact, everything in Christian experience springs from this fact. God has effected so real a spiritual union between us and Christ that He and we are one, sharing the very same life. Scripture asserts that we are in Him. This is not a truth arrived at by a process of logic; it is a revelation from God to be believed and acted on.

As if to reassure our unbelieving hearts that this is really true, several figures are used to illustrate and enforce it. Our Lord said, "I am the vine, ye are the branches" (John 15:5). The union between Christ and the believer is just as vital as that between the vine and the branch that shares its life. Paul says that we are members of the Body of Christ. Could there be closer union than that between the body and its members? Then there is the marital figure, the sweet intimacy and oneness which exist between husband and wife, which Paul uses to portray the intimacy of our union with Christ.

This union is a fact quite independent of our feelings about it. When we accept and believe the fact, it becomes a potent factor in our experience.

The verse quoted above further reveals that Christ to whom we have been thus united is made unto us wisdom—even righteousness and sanctification and redemption. When the queen bee lays an egg, there is deposited in the cell with it the food on which the larva is to feed during its development. Similarly, when God placed us "in Christ," He also made provision in Him for our whole life. Christ is made unto us wisdom to enable us to walk aright in a perplexing world, righteousness to replace our sinfulness, sanctification to impart the holiness we so greatly need, and redemption of the body to consummate the whole.

CHRIST IS IN US

"Know ye not . . . that Jesus Christ is in you . . . except ye be reprobates [counterfeit]?" (2 Cor. 13:5). Is it too elementary to point out that in this sentence Paul, writing by inspiration, said, "*Know* ye not," not "*Feel* ye not"? And yet the latter seems to be the sense in which many read this verse. This is *a fact to be counted on, not an experience to be sought.* Believe the fact and you will begin to enjoy the experience. The order cannot be reversed.

When Jesus was on earth, He was *with* His disciples, and for them this was a blessed and unforgettable experience. But in the upper room He said to them: "At that day ye shall know that . . . *I* [*am*] *in you*" (John 14:20)—an experience beyond anything they had known before. Although He was *with* His disciples until the day of His death, they still remained selfish, self-seeking, fearful, failing men.

In the days of His flesh Jesus could be in only one place at a time, and He could influence His disciples only from without. With the descent of the Holy Spirit on the Day of Pentecost, all this was changed. From that day Jesus knew no geographical limitations on account of His body. By His Spirit He could now dwell within each believer in every place and hold personal converse with each one. They lost His physical presence but gained His spiritual indwelling. Best of all, by His Spirit, He could now carry on His sanctifying work from within, from the center of the being.

Through ignorance or perhaps through ignoring this glorious truth, many Christians are still living in a pre-Pentecostal experience, knowing only an external Savior living in a distant heaven. They have never experienced the indwelling of Christ as a consciously enjoyed blessing. And yet it is an incontrovertible fact. "Know ye not that Jesus Christ *is* in you?" In some way which cannot be fully explained by human logic, the exalted Christ, by His Spirit, really indwells every true believer.

One great preacher to whom this truth came with all the power of a divine revelation said, "Oh, if every one of you will but keep saying to himself as I have done a hundred times a day: 'I do not feel it, I may not have the joy of it, but Jesus is as certainly in my heart as He is in heaven!' I say that a hundred times a day, and as I dare to affirm it, the Holy Spirit gives the manifestation of it."

The glorious fact is not to be apprehended merely intellectually. In Scriptural language we know it with our hearts. By way of illustration, the author is sitting in his study going over accounts. His wife is sitting alongside him doing some handwork. His whole mind is engrossed in his work. He is not thinking about his wife, for he cannot afford to think of anything else when he is adding up figures. Yet all the time he is conscious of her presence and enjoying her nearness. If she withdraws from the room he misses her and is glad when she returns. Yet all the time his mind is fully engaged elsewhere. It is somewhat in this sense that we can consciously be enjoying fellowship with the indwelling Christ while fully engaged in our daily work. "With your hearts ye shall know Him."

CHRIST FORMED IN YOU

In writing to the Galatian Christians, Paul said: "My little children, of whom I travail in birth again until *Christ be formed in you*" (Gal. 4:19). He had previously travailed for them until they had experienced the new birth, but he did not rest content with that. He did not want them to remain in a state of spiritual babyhood, but to go on to spiritual maturity.

It is one thing to have Christ *dwelling* in you by His Spirit, but quite another to have Christ *formed* in you. "Christ in you" became a fact in a moment, the moment you exercised saving faith in Christ. "Christ formed in you" is a process that continues for a lifetime.

The late Dr. F. B. Meyer illustrated this verse from the hatching of an egg. When the egg is laid, there floats in the midst of a sticky fluid the germ of the chick that is to be—the whole chick in embryo. It is a very little speck to start with, floating in a great quantity of viscous matter. But as the mother hen turns her eggs twice a day for three weeks there is less and less each day of the sticky matter and more and more of the chick that is being formed in the egg. One day there is no more viscous matter and all is chick. In exercise of the new life within, the chick chips its way out of the shell, and for it there begins the romance of life in an entirely new realm.

The picture is clear. How much there is in the best of us of the sticky self-life, and how little of Christ.

> O Jesus Christ, grow Thou in me,
>   And all things else recede;
> My heart be daily nearer Thee,
>   From sin be daily freed.
> —JOHANN CASPER LAVATER (1741–1801)

If we have been born again, then the germ of spiritual life is within. The new eternal life was imparted by the Holy Spirit at the moment of believing. But the new life entered only in embryo—a babe life that needs constant care and nurture. It was this that Peter had in mind when he counseled his readers: "As newborn babes, desire the sincere milk of the word, that ye may grow thereby" (1 Peter 2:2). As we gladly yield ourselves to the sanctifying influence of the Holy Spirit and reckon ourselves dead unto sin and alive unto God, we make it possible for Him to form Christ in us.

Theodore Monod describes the process in his hymn:

> Oh the bitter shame and sorrow,
>   That a time could ever be,
> When I let the Saviour's pity
> Plead in vain, and proudly answered,
>   "All of self, and none of Thee."
>
> Yet He found me; I beheld Him
>   Bleeding on the accursed tree,
> Heard Him pray, "Forgive them, Father,"
> And my wistful heart said faintly,
>   "Some of self, and some of Thee."
>
> Day by day His tender mercy,
>   Healing, helping, full and free,
> Sweet and strong, and ah! so patient,
> Brought me lower while I whispered,
>   "Less of self, and more of Thee."
>
> Higher than the highest heavens,
>   Deeper than the deepest sea,
> Lord, Thy love at last hath conquered;
> Grant me now my soul's petition,
>   "None of self, and all of Thee."
> —THEODORE MONOD (1836–1921)

How is the process of forming Christ within the believing life advanced? Every circumstance of our lives has been planned with this end in view. Our heredity and environment, our temperament, and all the frustrations and disappointments of life are not the result of blind chance. They are the careful planning of an omniscient and all-loving God. As we subject ourselves to the Word of God, the lordship of Christ, and the leading of the Spirit, the circumstances will combine to wean us from the old life of self-pleasing and to conform us to the image of Christ. Our Father loves us so well that He places us in positions of great difficulty and perplexity, withdraws some cherished object of love, places us to live and work with or among uncongenial people—all in order that we may despair of ourselves and learn to draw more on the resources which are for us in Christ.

The process of Christ being formed in us usually progresses more rapidly in times of adversity than in prosperity. When all runs smoothly, we tend to forget our dependence on God, but in times of trouble we turn to Him and appropriate His grace and help. Some of the greatest saints have been those who have been tested most severely. Received aright, the disciplines of life serve to reproduce in us the likeness of Christ.

Some years ago the author saw this illustrated to a remarkable degree in the life of a choice saint whom he visited in Melbourne, Australia. She had neither arms nor legs—just a pitiful trunk of a body. She had not moved from her room for forty-three years. She had not known during that time what it was to be free from pain. As he entered the cottage he noticed that she had named it "Gladwish." When he came into her presence, it was not to see a depressed invalid but rather a radiant, Christlike

Christian. To the end of the stump of an arm she had fastened a fountain pen. On the other stump she had a rubber attachment. With these she managed to manipulate a stand and a letter rack by her bedside. When the calamity overtook her, instead of rebelling against God, she took it from Him as a discipline intended to accelerate the formation of Christ in her.

She learned to write and began a correspondence that circled the globe. People began to visit in her little room, and no one left the room without being impressed with the triumph of Christ which she demonstrated.

She showed the author letters from people all over the world whom she had led to Christ, either in that little room or through her correspondence. Literally hundreds were brought to Christ through her fragrant ministry. The circumstances which might easily have crushed and embittered her served only to sweeten and make her more like her Master.

These three glorious facts are true of every genuine believer: You are in Christ. Christ is in you. Christ is being formed in you by the Holy Spirit. Let us yield ourselves without reserve to His mighty working until that process is complete, and at last we are fully conformed to the image of Christ.

8

Life Is Someone Else

For to me to live is Christ.

PHILIPPIANS 1:21

I live; yet not I, but Christ liveth in me.

GALATIANS 2:20

The indwelling of Christ in Paul was such a transforming experience that he could only sum it up in one pregnant sentence—"To me to live is Christ." To him, life was Someone else.

The title is rather intriguing, but does it make sense? What is meant by life? Can it be someone else? Is not my life peculiarly my own, something I must work out for myself?

A speaker at a large student conference circulated a questionnaire among the students requesting them to suggest the most important question in their thinking. Of the four most popular topics, "What is the meaning of life?"

came first. Science cannot tell us. Philosophy can make an important contribution to the answer, but it can give no finality. There is no final satisfying answer outside the Christian revelation, and in the Scriptures millions of sane and intelligent people have found the answer to their quest.

WHAT IS LIFE?

It is a mystery both as to its source and origin, apart from the Christian revelation. Science has been unable to wrest its secret from its Author, who keeps it locked up in His own breast. It defies analysis and is difficult to define. One definition is that life is the ability to correspond to environment. But this is only partially satisfactory. It recognizes no original source of activity within, but only a power of reaction to stimulus from without.

Life is the chief theme of the New Testament, and the word occurs over one thousand times. Frequently it is "eternal life," an expression which signifies much more than mere endlessness. It is a term of quality rather than of duration. A nearer approach to a definition occurs in our Lord's prayer, "*This is life eternal*, that they might know thee the only true God, and Jesus Christ, whom thou hast sent" (John 17:3). Knowledge is more than intellectual conception. It is moral knowledge, personal acquaintance, inner affinity, and sympathy. It involves experiencing similar emotions and interchanging deepest feelings with God and Christ. "*This is life eternal*," in all its fullness. Life's fullness is never experienced when out of harmony with Christ.

People young and old are frankly disappointed with life.

It has not yielded them what they have craved, and they are disillusioned and frustrated. Goethe, for example, said: "I have been deemed, and I believe justly, one of fortune's favorites. Yet I cannot, as I look back on my life, recall more than three weeks of positive happiness in the whole." This may be rather an extreme case and yet it is by no means an isolated one. A whole generation of young people could make a similar confession.

By way of contrast, hear Paul's testimony: "I am now ready to be offered, and the time of my departure is at hand. I have fought a good fight, I have finished my course, I have kept the faith: Henceforth there is laid up for me a crown of righteousness, which the Lord, the righteous judge, shall give me at that day" (2 Tim. 4:6–8). There is no disillusionment or frustration here. He had lived life to the full, had worked hard and suffered much, but at the end it was satisfaction, fulfillment, reward.

If Paul were challenged and asked what made him what he was, and what had enabled him to triumph in such painful and adverse circumstances, he might have replied: "Once I could describe my life like this: To me to live is *Paul*. But since I saw the vision on the Damascus road, the center of my life has shifted. Now to me to live is *Christ*." To him life was now Someone else.

It is a searching spiritual exercise to ask and answer the question: "To me to live is _____?"

There must be some center, some unifying motive to our lives. What is it, self or Christ? Hear Paul again: "I live, yet no longer I—*Christ liveth in me*" (paraphrase). Whatever else he meant, he was saying that since his conversion the center of life had shifted from him to Someone else, and that change had changed the circumference as well.

It is told of Mahmoud, who conquered a great portion of India hundreds of years ago that he destroyed all the idols in every town to which he came. He laid siege to the great city of Guzurat. Forcing for himself an entrance into the costliest shrine of the Brahmans, there rose before him the figure of a gigantic idol, fifteen feet high. He instantly ordered it to be destroyed. The Brahmans of the temple prostrated themselves at his feet and said: "Great Mahmoud, spare our god, for the fortunes of this city depend on him."

> Ransom vast of gold they offer, pearls of
>   price and jewels rare,
> Purchase of their idol's safety, this their
>   dearest will he spare.
> And there wanted not who counselled, that
>   he should his hand withhold,
> Should that single image suffer, and
>   accept the proffered gold.
> —RICHARD CHENEVIX TRENCH

But Mahmoud, after a moment's pause, said he would rather be known as the breaker than the seller of idols, and struck the image with his battle-ax. His soldiers followed, and in an instant the idol was broken to pieces. It proved to be hollow and had been used as a receptacle for thousands

of precious gems which, as the image was shattered, fell at
the conqueror's feet.

> From its shattered side revealing pearls
>   and diamonds, showers of gold;
> More than all that proffered ransom, more
>   than all a hundred fold.

Such an idol is self, pleading eloquently to be spared
and offering in return pleasures and treasures untold. But
when Paul, ignoring self's plea, learned the secret of losing
his life for Christ's sake, he found true wealth and pleasure.
The Christ against whom he had directed his rage and
venom now possessed and energized his whole personality
in such a way that he could only describe it as Christ living in him. What is the talisman enfolded in these simple
words: "To me to live is Christ"?

Christ was the Source of his life. "I am . . . the life," said the
Son of God (John 14:6). "Christ, who is our life," said Paul
(Col. 3:4). Jesus said: "I am come that they might have life,
and . . . have it more abundantly" (John 10:10). Christ does
not impart life as something separate from Himself. When a
heart is opened to Him in true repentance and surrender, He
Himself comes in and communicates His own life. "He that
hath the Son hath life" (1 John 5:12). And it is abundant life
that is in view—not that of an emaciated convalescent in the
hospital but of a virile youth on the football field.

Christ was the Mediator of his spiritual life. "I live; yet
not I, but Christ liveth in me" (Gal. 2:20). If his words
mean anything, they mean that the Christian life is Christ

living out His pure, holy, and wholesome life in terms of our human life and personality. The new life which a person receives at regeneration, or the new birth, is not an abstraction. It is not a spiritual dynamic or energy, but the indwelling of a divine Person. Christianity is not a creed to live by. It is a Person who indwells. Christianity is Christ.

Christ living in us will *stimulate and not stultify the intellect*. The intellect in its natural state is astray on spiritual things. With the advent of Christ into the personality, the mind is able to comprehend and apprehend spiritual truths and realities. Truths which previously had been mysterious glow with heavenly light.

Christ living in us will *quicken the affections and emotional life* and fix them on God, the ethically perfect Being, in whom we will find the fullest satisfaction.

Christ living in us will *vitalize the will* which has become weakened and emasculated by habitual yielding to sinful impulses.

This is exactly what happened to Paul. His bitter hatred for Christ and His church turned to blazing and sacrificial love. The whole energy of his brilliant intellect and dynamic will was concentrated on making amends for the havoc he had made of the church and the grief he had brought to Christ. He gave himself to the winning of others to Christ, who had captured him.

It must be observed that Christ will never forcibly intrude into a human personality. He will bring every influence to bear upon a life, short of violating the personality. Before Paul's conversion, Christ was anathema to him. But when, in the blaze of heavenly revelation on the Damascus road, he recognized Christ's claims and surrendered to Him, that very moment his whole being was indwelt and irradiated by Christ. So real was this experience that Paul could only describe it in the cryptic sentence—"To me to live is Christ."

Paul's personality was not obliterated by that indwelling. "*I live*," he said, "yet not I, but Christ liveth in me." He did not become any the less Paul because he was indwelt by Christ. Indeed, he became more and more the Paul God intended him to be; the ideal Paul who was a chosen vessel to the Lord. We need not fear the fullest surrender to Christ, for He enhances and ennobles personality. He imparts qualities which are absent and brings into activity powers and possibilities which were latent. He became a different Paul, but a greater and a better Paul. Apart from the indwelling and mastery of Christ, the world would probably have heard little of him. Instead his influence has been one of the dominating features of the last two millennia.

Christ lived in Paul in the sense that from within the citadel of his yielded personality He reproduced His own gracious and radiant life. Through his letters, while it was characteristically Paul who wrote, and the letters bore all the marks of his personality, Christ was able to convey His message to successive generations of Christians.

Through constant communion with Christ, Paul became less and less like the Saul of his persecuting days and more and more like the Christ with whom he companied. He lived a life which emanated from the same Source, was inspired by the same ideals, governed by the same standards, and enabled by the same power as his indwelling Lord. To him, life indeed was Someone else.

9

Cultivation of
Christian Character

Giving all diligence, add to your faith . . .

2 PETER 1:5

The indwelling of Christ is an act of God's grace in which we have no part. The sanctifying work of the Holy Spirit is sovereign, but it will progress only insofar as we cooperate with Him. There is a human as well as a divine part in the cultivation of Christian character.

It is not always easy to discern where God's part in the work of sanctification ends and where man's begins. There is something which God alone can do, and something which man alone can do. In this paragraph, Peter is dealing with the human factor in the cultivation of Christian character. He indicates that it does not develop automatically; Christian character does not just happen. We have a contribution to make to our own sanctification. Paul indicates this too. "Work out your own salvation with fear and trembling," he wrote to the Philippian believers. But he did not stop there, but continued, "*for* it is God which worketh in you both to will and to do of his good pleasure" (Phil. 2:12–13). We are able to work out the salvation which is ours by faith, because the Holy Spirit is at work in us supplying the impulse and enabling the performance.

Peter reminds his readers of three factors which make Christian character attainable and form the basis of our moral endeavor. He is emphasizing what God has done in every believer. (1) The bestowal of everything necessary for a wholesome and godly life. "His divine power hath given unto us all things that pertain unto life and godliness" (2 Peter 1:3). (2) The granting of promises which are great and beyond all price—"exceeding great and precious promises" (v. 4). (3) The impartation of His own very nature—"that by these ye might be partakers of the divine nature" (v. 4).

If these words mean anything, they mean that we have at our disposal the limitless resources of God. These have been placed to our credit in the bank of heaven. That is God's part. But we must draw and present the checks. He cannot do that for us.

Peter goes on to urge that the possession of this limitless spiritual wealth, so freely given, should stir us to the diligent cultivation of that Christian character which was seen in perfection in Christ. Verse 5 has been correctly translated, "*For this very reason*, make every effort to supplement your faith with virtue." Divine grace must be supplemented by human endeavor. It is God who provides the seed, the soil, the sun, and the rain, but it requires the diligent cooperation of the farmer to produce a good crop.

THE NECESSITY FOR DILIGENCE

Peter was of the active, motor type who must be always doing something, so it is appropriate for him to urge diligence. The Greek word rendered "diligence" is much more colorful. It implies haste begotten by earnestness, and involves the idea of serious moral endeavor. Peter wanted to see every minute crowded with earnest effort. There are many passages emphasizing this aspect of truth. "Let us *labor* . . . to enter into that rest" (Heb. 4:11). "*Not slothful* in business" (Rom. 12:11). "*Study* to shew thyself approved unto God" (2 Tim. 2:15). There is a difference between haste and hurry. The latter may be caused by dilatoriness and lack of discipline and have no purpose in view.

We are to be diligent, for our ingrained tendency is to be slack. Some who are very diligent in making money lack a similar earnestness in divine things. The shortness of time and the brevity of life should lead us to bend all our energies and employ all our powers in cultivating Christian character.

QUALITIES INVOLVED IN DILIGENCE

There are three ideas implied in the word "diligence." (1) *Earnestness*, enthusiasm, zeal. We are to bend our hearts and minds to our objective. Our Lord possessed this quality. He said, "The zeal of thine house hath eaten me up" (John 2:17). We must throw all we have into the building of Christlike character. (2) *Industry*. This is the most serious work to which we can give ourselves. There is no progress without industry. Holiness never thrives on neglected duties. It is true that our sanctification, like our justification, is by faith. But it is a faith which inspires human endeavor. God has made our sanctification possible by the death and resurrection of His Son and the gift of the Holy Spirit. We can add nothing to that. But God will not study the Bible or pray for us! He will not witness to others for us. There is a part to which we must industriously give ourselves. God will not give us good habits. We must cultivate them. (3) *Perseverance*, persistence. Victory comes to the one who perseveres to the end. It is easy to lose heart and give up when spiritual progress seems slow. There is an Eastern proverb which says that there are only two creatures that can surmount the pyramids, the eagle and the snail. In our pursuit of character we should combine the venturesomeness of the eagle and the tenacity of the snail.

THE SUBJECTS OF OUR DILIGENCE

Our faith is to be supplemented by seven graces which are essential to a well-balanced character. The word "add" has a vivid background. It was a word used in connection with Greek plays, all of which required large choruses, and these were very expensive to maintain. Public-spirited citizens would volunteer to equip and maintain a chorus, and would do it on a very lavish scale. It is to be our objective, not to get away with the barest minimum of Christian character, but to aim at having our lives adorned with every lovely grace;

to be content with nothing less than a splendid life. God will not give us character, but He has provided in Christ and the Holy Spirit all we require to become increasingly like Christ.

It is to be noted that in these seven graces *faith* is the foundation and *love* is the culmination. Every grace in between springs out of faith and is to be expressed in love. All seven graces are to be reproduced in each Christian. We are not to be specialists in one grace and neglect others.

We are to supplement our faith with:

1. Virtue—that virile, manly strength which inspires to resolute action. It carries the idea of excellence, virtue in every sense. It is not merely a passive quality but issues in a life of courageous witness and effective service for God. It is the inflexible determination to do right and choose God's will, no matter how strongly the tide is running in the opposite direction.

2. Knowledge—not theoretical knowledge only, but practical knowledge born out of personal experience. It refers not to general culture, nor even to intellectual knowledge of theological truth. It is insight into what is right and what is wrong, and discernment of how we ought to act in the light of what we know. It is knowledge which enables correct decisions and efficient action.

3. Self-control—the ability to rule oneself, body and spirit. It extends over the whole life—emotions, passions, desires, imaginations. Jeremy Taylor described self-control as "reason's girdle as well as passion's bridle." Our bodily appetites which are part of our human nature are beneficent when controlled but ruinous when in command. But strong though they are, they can be controlled

by the indwelling Holy Spirit whose fruit is temperance, or self-control (Gal. 5:23). Apart from His enabling, one part of our nature cannot control another part which is in revolt. Our passions and desires are not removed at conversion, but we can bring them under perpetual mastery through the Holy Spirit.

Frances Ridley Havergal, the saintly hymn writer, as a young woman had a fiery temper which again and again brought her to despair. After one outburst she had a transaction with God about it, and trusted the Holy Spirit to give deliverance. Her sister testified that never again did she lose her temper.

4. Patience—a grace in which there are two elements: active perseverance and passive endurance. Our idea of patience is usually stolid endurance, but this is far from the meaning of the word here. It is that spirit which not only endures but actually triumphs over trials and turns them into glorious victories. William Barclay tells of Beethoven that when he was threatened by deafness, instead of lapsing into despair, the great composer said, "I will take life by the throat." And everyone knows that some of his greatest works were written after he became deaf. Someone said to a woman who was in the midst of great sorrow, "Sorrow does color life, doesn't it?" "Yes, and I propose to choose the colors," was the reply. This is the idea behind patience in this passage. It is not sitting down to endure but rising up and using every adverse experience as a stepping-stone to the achievement of some higher purpose.

5. Godliness—true reverence for God, or reverential trust. This is not a quality which is innate even in the

Christian. It must be cultivated. It results in both God and man receiving their due from us. Paul exhorted Timothy to exercise himself unto godliness, and the word he used refers to the strenuous training of an athlete for his race. If we are determined to be godly, we must be willing to pay the price in self-discipline, for it does not just happen.

6. Brotherly love—our badge of discipleship. "By this shall all men know that ye are my disciples, if ye have love one to another" (John 13:35). Because we have the same Father, we should cultivate a warm affection for one another. If we do not recognize the obligations of brotherhood, we place ourselves in the category of the elder brother of Luke 15.

7. Love—the crown and culmination of all. It is the queen of all graces. It has been defined as "the sovereign preference of one person for another." Our Lord claimed the supreme place in the affections of His followers. Love of parent for child and of husband for wife must be secondary to love for Him, or else we cannot be His disciples. But when this is truly conceded, there is an abundance of love in the heart which can overflow in all directions and to all men. The love of God is shed abroad in our hearts by the Holy Spirit. This is one of the greatest needs in the world of today—a manifestation of the love of God toward men and women who are weighed down by sorrow and suffering.

So then, in this ideal of Christian character which Peter depicts for us, faith is the root and love is the fruit. In between are the other graces which round out the whole. If these qualities increasingly abound in us, our lives will be neither barren nor unfruitful, and we ourselves will be constantly growing in our knowledge of the Master.

Is this not an objective worthy of our every endeavor? Is it not worth "giving all diligence"?

10

The Wiles of the Devil

Put on the whole armour of God, that ye may be
able to stand against the wiles of the devil.

EPHESIANS 6:11

The development of Christian character is not automatic. The believer who longs for a holy life will find
himself resisted at every point by a wily and unscru-
pulous foe. But he has no cause to be terrified by his
adversary.

There is a tendency in the contemporary world to dis-
count our Lord's teaching concerning the existence
of a personal devil. Instead of there being a personal God
and a personal devil, many say there is only impersonal
good and evil. But the language used in Scripture cannot
be made to fit an impersonal force or influence. There is a
uniform conception of a personal tempter able to inflame
the base tendencies of our hearts with his incitements to
evil. In the scriptural view the devil is the personification of

evil as God is the personification of all that is holy.

The theme of the Bible is the conflict between God and the devil, the clash of the hierarchy of heaven with the hierarchy of hell. The key to an understanding of the world situation is the recognition that these two thrones are at war. Satan's objective is nothing less than the elimination of God and the usurping of His throne.

HIS PERSON AND CHARACTER

Christ used three vivid words to describe *his person*. *Satan* means, "adversary, opposer." Although the word is not always used of an evil enemy, in Hebrew literature it is always reserved for the devil, the enemy of all that is holy, the opposer of all that is good. Our Lord used this name in the pregnant statement: "I beheld Satan as lightning fall from heaven" (Luke 10:18), a statement consistent with the view that he was a created intelligence. Originally the guardian of the throne of God, he was banished from the divine presence because of his unbridled and unholy ambition to oust God from His throne.

He is called *the devil*, meaning "slanderer, traducer, false accuser." This name always conveys the idea of evil. He slandered God to Adam and slandered Job to God. Slander is still one of his most potent and universal weapons, and he is never more pleased than when he can incite saints to use it against other saints.

Jesus referred to him as *Beelzebub*, the master of flies. The idea seems to be that he is the genius who presides over corruption. Everything he does is corrupting and corroding. He pollutes thought and word and act, and aims to spoil all that is pure and holy.

Several other words are employed to delineate his character. He is *the prince of this world*, a title indicating his mastery over mankind. He rules evil men as well as evil spirits. "We know that . . . the whole world lies under the dominance of the wicked one," wrote John (1 John 5:19 MLB). The underlying picture is that of the world lying unconscious in his arms. The rebel prince is determined to prevent the establishment of Christ's kingdom over men, and to achieve this end he uses every method, fair or foul.

He is described as a *murderer*. He began his foul task in the first human family, and has perpetuated it ever since through crime and war.

He is a *liar*, and the father of lies. He falsifies the truth, misrepresents the character of God, and deceives and deludes the saints.

As the *dragon*, he is represented as a malicious and hostile personality, implacably set on the destruction of man. As *that old serpent*, his craft and cunning are emphasized. He is *an angel of light*, concealing his malignity under a guise of benignity.

HIS STRATEGY

Victor Hugo said that a good general must penetrate the brain of his enemy. Paul recognized this truth and endeavored to arouse those to whom he wrote of this necessity. Today it must be acknowledged that on this subject the majority of Christians are spiritual illiterates, and nothing pleases the adversary more than our ignorance of his strategy and wiles.

His overall strategy is to supersede and overthrow the kingdom of God. It is a strategy of destruction. If he was too clever for man in his perfection in Eden, he has a much greater advantage over man in his fallen state.

It has been said that he plans *to destroy human government through anarchy*. Any student of history can trace this stratagem of the devil, the pervading activity of a malign power, poisoning the stream of human history. He is the mastermind behind the present world system with its lust for power and its political and economic intrigue.

He purposes *to destroy human society through debauchery*. Any student of sociology can trace a similar pattern in the cycles of human history. In our own day we have seen the world flooded with moral filth to a degree inconceivable fifty years ago.

He aims *to destroy true religion through apostasy*. Any student of theology and church history can discern recurring heresies and apostasies through the centuries. And in our own day there has been a widespread recrudescence of many of the old heresies in the heretical cults which have been spawned and are now encircling the globe.

As the god of this age, he has set up a complete counterfeit of Christianity. Not without reason did Augustine term him *Simius Dei*, the ape of God. He has his own *trinity*—the devil, the beast, and the false prophet; his own church—the synagogue of Satan (Rev. 2:9); his own ministers—ministers of Satan (2 Cor. 11:15); his own gospel—another gospel (Gal. 1:6); his own theology—doctrines of devils (1 Tim. 4:1); his own sacrifices—sacrifices offered to demons (1 Cor. 10:20); his own table and cup (1 Cor. 10:21–22).

Everything about him is false. He uses false and counterfeit instruments to achieve his purpose. He employs *false teachers* (Acts 20:30; 2 Peter 2:1) who specialize in his theology and "bring in damnable heresies." They creep privily into the churches and subtly mix truth with error. He enlists the support of *false prophets* (2 Peter 2:1; Matt. 24:11). Professing to have a message from God, they in reality draw their inspiration from hell. He promotes *false Christs* (Matt. 24:4–5), self-constituted messiahs and deliverers. He is aided by *false apostles*, deceitful workers (2 Cor. 11, 13), and *false brethren* (Gal. 2:4–5) who steal in to spy out the liberty of believers, in order to draw them back into legal bondage.

Paul sums up this aspect of the devil's activities in these words: "And no marvel; for Satan himself is transformed into an angel of light. Therefore it is no great thing if his ministers also be transformed as the ministers of righteousness; whose end shall be according to their works" (2 Cor. 11:14–15).

HIS WILES

Paul used two words in this connection. The first is "devices" (2 Cor. 2:11), which signifies thoughts, sophistical reasonings. The second, "wiles," means "method" or "strategy" (Eph. 6:11). It is used of the skill one observes in the handling of a point in an argument, or the intellectual ingenuity involved in composing an ordered discourse. It is thus a fitting word for the devil's expertise in his warfare against the Christian.

He seduces into sin, beguiles and fascinates his prey. To do this he chooses occasions when his temptation is most likely to be entertained. His temptation to discouragement came to Elijah when he was overwrought and overspent. The temptation to denial came to Peter when hopes and aspirations had been shattered. The temptation to lust struck David at a time of illegitimate relaxation. Joseph was tempted by Potiphar's wife when there were no men in the house. The devil is essentially a coward who delights to strike when we are weak in body or low in spirits. He uses the hour of death to launch some of his fiercest attacks.

Then, too, he selects the most suitable instruments of temptation. Adam received the fatal fruit from his wife's hand. When Jonah was tempted to flee from the divine commission to preach to Nineveh, he found the ship bound for Tarshish ready at hand.

He disables the warrior and endeavors to put him out of the battle. Old sins which God has forgiven and forgotten are raked up with startling vividness. Old William Gurnall once said of the devil: "He lays his brats at the saint's door and then charges him with that which is his own creation." He discourages the warrior in the midst of the battle and endeavors to bring him to despair.

He deceives the saints, even the very elect, luring them into sin or leading them into error. He uses a wide variety of methods.

He sows tares among the wheat, plants the children of

the wicked one among the children of God. Like tares, they are indistinguishable in the early stages, but later cause great trouble in the church. *He lays snares*, traps for the unwary, into which they fall when out of close touch with God. *He sows dissension* among believers. He began with the first family. He did the same in the early church. He injects the poison of suspicion, jealousy, criticism, intolerance, and fosters misunderstandings which lead to fragmentation and division. *He snatches away the good seed* as soon as it is sown. *He persecutes* or *flatters* the church, whichever seems more likely to succeed.

On the mission fields of the world his activities are equally varied. He endeavors to secure the expulsion of missionaries. He uses the pressures of heathen culture to compel the worship of demons or worship at the shrine of ancestors. He deflects missionaries from true gospel activity into secondary though good pursuits. He injects false teaching, divides evangelical forces, dries up sources of funds for missionary work, drives missionaries to unduly feverish activity, and "wears out the saints."

Perhaps this analysis will enable us to pierce the brain of our enemy to some degree.

DEFENSE AND OFFENSE

To write thus of the enormous power and subtlety of our adversary, and of the intensity of the warfare he wages, without mentioning *Calvary*, is like writing of the Napoleonic wars without mention of Waterloo.

It is true that:

> His power and craft are great,
> And armed with cruel hate,
> On earth is not his equal.
> —MARTIN LUTHER (1483–1546); translated by Frederick
> H. Hedge (1805–1890)

But in heaven, seated at the right hand of God, is One who is more than a match for him. Speaking to the seventy disciples who returned from their evangelistic crusade, rejoicing that even the demons were subject to them through His name, Jesus said: "I beheld Satan as lightning fall from heaven. *Behold, I give unto you power . . . over all the power of the enemy*" (Luke 10:18–19).

This passage places the emphasis not on the power of the enemy, but on the possibility of victory through the delegated power of Christ. Christ vanquished him at the Cross, and invites us to share His victory. Here was the explanation of the apostles' victory over Satan. There had first been a victory in the spiritual realm which accounted for their victory and success in their evangelizing ministry. "Having spoiled principalities and powers, he made a shew of them openly, triumphing over them in it" (Col. 2:15).

> The foe is stern and eager,
>   The fight is fierce and long;
> But Thou hast made us mighty
>   And stronger than the strong.
> —W. CHATTERTON DIX (1867)

Lest we be "terrified by our adversaries," it is well to remember that Satan's power is not inherent but permitted (Rom. 13:1). It is not unlimited, but controlled (Job 1:12; 2:6). It is not invincible, but broken (Luke 11:21–22). It is not assured of success, but is surely doomed (Rev. 20:2–3). Satan knows well that there is no ultimate victory for him. The pronounced sentence has only been postponed. But he works to hinder and postpone Christ's final triumph. We can rejoice in the certainty of John's assurance: "Greater is he that is in you, than he that is in the world" (1 John 4:4).

11

Warfare and Weapons

For the weapons of our warfare are
not carnal, but mighty through God
to the pulling down of strong holds.

2 CORINTHIANS 10:4

The Spirit-filled Christian is not concerned merely with
his own spiritual experience. He realizes that he is in
the midst of a truceless warfare. He must learn what
his weapons are and how to use them effectively.

In his classic *The Holy War*, John Bunyan wrote,
"Mansoul's matchless wars no fables be." He was very
conscious of the truceless warfare in which every true fol-
lower of the Lamb is inevitably engaged.

> I saw the Prince's armed men come down
> By troops, by thousands, to besiege the town;
> I saw the captains, heard the trumpets sound,
> And how his forces covered all the ground.

Yea, how they set themselves in battle-'ray
I shall remember to my dying day.
    I saw the colours waving in the wind,
    And they within to mischief how combin'd
To ruin Mansoul.

Few who have been engaged in spiritual warfare, especially in heathen lands, will be disposed to quarrel with Bunyan's picture. A review of Christian missions down the centuries reveals that every significant advance has been matched by special opposition from the adversary. The form and method have varied with the time and circumstances, but the warfare has been directed by a brilliant and wily strategist.

There are those who doubt the existence of a personal and malignant devil, but the *fact* of the battle proves the existence of the foe, and the *fierceness* of the fight is an index of his might. The disciple must remember that he belongs to the church militant which is engaged in ceaseless warfare against the powers of darkness.

THE WARFARE

The word "campaign" is a more accurate translation of the Greek word than "warfare." There is a great difference between a battle and a campaign. In a campaign it is the last battle that is important. Battles can be lost and yet the campaign won, as in the Libyan Desert during World War II.

The warfare is *real*, not imaginary. His encounter with the devil was very real to Jesus, and the conflict was not confined to the forty days in the wilderness. It did not conclude until He shouted, "It is finished." If there is no conflict with the devil in our lives, we are either unsaved or have chosen to be noncombatants. The warfare is indeed no fable.

The warfare is *spiritual*, not carnal. "We do not war after the flesh." It is not waged on the plane or after the methods of the natural man. "Although of course we lead normal human lives, the battle we are fighting is on the spiritual level" is Phillips's rendering of verse 3. Methods which would avail in ordinary warfare are ineffective in this campaign. It can be waged only on the spiritual plane and only with spiritual weapons.

The warfare is *intangible*, "not against flesh and blood." It would be much more satisfying if we could grapple with our foe. There is some satisfaction in making contact. But the enemy we fight is not tangible. We cannot seize people and drag them from his clutch, much as we would like to do it. We cannot shake people into sanctification. We can reach and move them only by spiritual means. Carnal methods produce carnal results. The warfare we wage is one of ideologies and ideas, of words and prayers.

The warfare is *interminable*. It began in Eden and will end only when Satan is finally bound. As god of this world, he is fighting to retain control of the world and its men. He is fighting to destroy the church. It is an unending struggle to defend the heart against his subtle infiltration and sudden assaults. It is a warfare from which there is no discharge.

THE BATTLEFIELD—IMAGINATIONS AND THOUGHTS

Every battle has its strategic focal point on which forces and guns must be concentrated until it is reduced. In the battle of Waterloo, the battle flowed around a farmhouse on an eminence on the battlefield. In World War I, Hill 60 was the focal point. In World War II the focal point changed, as the fighting was more fluid. Now it was El Alamein, and now the Coral Sea.

In our spiritual warfare, the battle rages around the citadel of the mind. It is fought in the realm of thought and imagination. The mind stands midway between the body and the spirit and mediates what comes from either. It can be dominated and controlled by the flesh or by the Spirit, by God or by Satan. On one memorable occasion Peter, dominated by the Holy Spirit, made the great confession: "Thou art the Christ, the Son of the living God." Shortly after, the same Peter endeavored unwittingly to deflect Jesus from the way of the cross and earned the solemn rebuke: "Get thee behind me, Satan." It is tragically possible for the same tongue to be controlled by either the Spirit or by Satan. And it is I who decide which shall be in control.

Paul indicates three areas that are involved:

Imagination, or reasonings, theories (2 Cor. 10:5). Evil imaginations led to the judgment of the flood. "God saw that the wickedness of man was great in the earth, and that every imagination of the thoughts of his heart was only evil continually. . . . and the LORD said, I will destroy man . . . from the face of the earth" (Gen. 6:5, 7). The race had degenerated and lost the knowledge of God and, as a result, became "vain in their imaginations." The imagination can be either a bane or a blessing. A sanctified imagination is an inestimable boon to a preacher. But it can also be a fruitful source of sin. It conjures up desires and images that are wrong and impure. When the will toys with these evil imaginations instead of rejecting them, they capture the thought processes and the citadel falls. Where there is a contest between the imagination and the will, the former is invariably victorious.

Thoughts (v. 5). This word is the same as "devices" in chapter 2, verse 11, and signifies plans and purposes. The Scriptures indicate that men's minds are in a state of rebellion, at enmity with God. Our thoughts and philosophies, our plans and purposes are contrary to God's. "My thoughts are not your thoughts," the Lord said. They tend naturally in the opposite direction, and Satan plays on that fact which he knows so well.

Every high thing that exalteth itself against the knowledge of God (v. 5). Knox translates it "every barrier of pride," every stronghold that towers high in defiance of the knowledge of God. It is a military figure. Instead of humbly submitting to God's wisdom and knowledge, man in his intellectual pride erects the ramparts of his own philosophies and speculations. There is no greater enemy to the spread of the knowledge of God than godless as opposed to true intellectualism. This is the intangible territory on which the warfare is waged, and Paul's aim is to demolish every such stronghold.

THE TACTICS

"Casting down imaginations." "Bringing into captivity every thought to the obedience of Christ."

"I demolish theories," is Moffatt's rendering—every

deceptive fantasy. The teaching of heretical cults would certainly come within the scope of this warfare. We are not counseled to demolish reason, that God-given faculty, but the reasonings which rob Christ of His throne and God of His glory. These philosophical fortifications are to be razed to the ground. But how? By the proclamation of truth. This is the only certain way of counteracting error.

"I make each rebel purpose my prisoner of war, and bow it in submission to Christ," is A. S. Way's rendering of verse 5. It is a devastatingly inclusive statement—every thought, purpose, plan is to be brought under Christ's sovereign sway. Every fugitive thought is to be brought into total obedience to Christ. And the reason is that if I do not thus bring my thoughts voluntarily under His control, they will be at the mercy of external and infernal influences. This cannot be achieved without a definite and persistent purpose and trustful dependence on the Holy Spirit.

THE WEAPONS

"The weapons of our warfare are not carnal," not those of human warfare. What are these spiritual weapons?

The Cross. We pay lip service to the cross, and even wear it as a talisman or symbol. But do we use it as a spiritual weapon? Do we know its mighty severing and conquering power? Do we pay more attention to our organization, methods, techniques, and legislation than to the irresistible dynamic of the cross? When facing spiritual problems and crises, do we rely more on conference than on the cross? Do we bring the cross onto the field?

There is nothing the devil fears so much as the intelligent appropriation and application of the power which was generated and released by the cross and resurrection of our Lord. He will do all in his power to divert us from wielding this weapon in the secret place of prayer. Paul learned his lesson. "I determined not to know any thing among you," he said, "save Jesus Christ, and him crucified" (1 Cor. 2:2). "The preaching [word] of the cross is . . . the power [dynamite] of God" (1 Cor. 1:18). He refused to preach the gospel "with wisdom of [man's] words, lest the cross of Christ should be made of none effect" (1 Cor. 1:17). Here is the acid test of all preaching. It is to be not in the wisdom of men but in the power of the cross.

The Truth. This is a weapon which, wielded in faith and in the power of the Spirit, will reduce the stoutest stronghold of sin and error. The adversary has no answer to the truth of God. The best he can do is to attempt to prevent it from reaching the minds of his captives. "The god of this world hath blinded the minds of them which believe not, lest the light of the glorious gospel of Christ . . . should shine unto them" (2 Cor. 4:4). The entrance of divine truth into the heart gives light and dispels erroneous conceptions. It is as a sword, discerning and discovering the thoughts and intents of the heart. It is like a hammer, demolishing resistance.

All Prayer. In Paul's classic passage on the spiritual warfare and the armor of the Christian warrior, he concludes: "Praying always with all prayer and supplication in the Spirit, and watching thereunto with all perseverance and supplication for all saints" (Eph. 6:18). We are to engage in prayer of every kind, whether worship, confession, thanksgiving, supplication, or intercession. Especially must we engage in that kind of prayer which claims and releases the power of the cross and which employs all the resources which are ours by virtue of our union with Christ. It is prayer which gives an edge to the truth. It is prayer which will open blind eyes to the truth which the god of this world is endeavoring to obscure. It is prayer which will prepare the soil of the heart so that when the truth is heard, it will fall into good ground, and bring forth fruit.

"The weapons of our warfare are . . . mighty through God to the pulling down of strong holds."

12

Evidences of True Spirituality

When thou prayest, enter into thy closet.

MATTHEW 6:6

In the Sermon on the Mount, our Lord indicated three areas in which true spirituality would manifest itself, and some motives which would rob them of any value.

In this section of the Sermon on the Mount (Matt. 6:1–18), our Lord vividly contrasted the hypocrisy of the Pharisees with the sincerity and true spirituality He expected in His disciples. He warned of the peril of self-advertisement and urged the maintenance in private of the kind of life they professed to live in public. He selected three ways in which the spiritual life manifests itself and showed how each of them could be hollow and valueless because of a wrong underlying motive. In each case He cited, the underlying motive was that their professed spirituality might be seen of men in public, and this motive entirely vitiated the commendable thing that had been done.

SPIRITUAL GENEROSITY (VV. 1–4)

It is to be noted that Jesus expected the giving of alms to be normal practice. He said, "When thou doest thine alms," not "if." The method of the hypocrites was to trumpet their almsgiving and draw attention to their generosity. It was the ancient equivalent of the modern subscription list. The gifts were given not for the benefit of the poor but for the personal aggrandizement of the donor; not to bring glory to God but to obtain glory from men. "Verily . . . they have"— or better—"have had their reward," said Jesus. The word is used of giving a receipt in full settlement. The hypocrite, or play-actor as the word means, had already received what he sought, the glory of men, and there was no more coming to him. His gift had not been transmuted into heavenly currency. He had laid up no treasure in heaven.

Some Christians look on giving to God as an investment, as a paying proposition. That great Christian philanthropist, Robert G. Le Tourneau, correctly said, "If you give to God because it pays, it won't pay." The motive is wrong. True spiritual generosity is without publicity or self-advertisement and for the glory of God alone. Otherwise there is no credit for it.

There has sometimes been a misunderstanding of the injunction that we are not to let our right hand know what our left hand does (Matt. 6:3). This has been interpreted by some teachers as requiring that all our giving should be done anonymously and almost secretively. The key to the correct interpretation of the verse lies in the fact that there are two words for "know." One means knowledge gained from information imparted. The other signifies knowledge gained by perception. It is the first word which Jesus used. We must not draw attention to our generosity. There is no objection to the gift being known to others who learn about it without our drawing attention to it, provided that is not the motive which prompts it. The spiritual Christian neither flaunts his giving nor talks about it to others. But it is right that men "may see your good works and glorify your Father which is in heaven." It is wrong for us to inform them of our good works so that we may receive their praise.

A wealthy and godly church member thought this verse meant that no one should know of his giving. He made a practice of making a large gift to the church each year, strictly anonymously. He never put any gift in the offering plate, because others would see it. He earned the name of being a skinflint. Instead of his action bringing glory to God, it harmed His cause and robbed the man of fellowship with others.

When Barnabas made a gift of his land to the Lord, he did it openly and all knew of it. It was an open and healthy transaction. God was glorified. Barnabas and the church were blessed. In the case of Ananias and Sapphira, it was ostentatious and hypocritical, and the result was not blessing but judgment. At the same time there can be a preciousness, a luxury in giving, when only God knows.

SPIRITUAL PRAYING (VV. 5–15)

Again it is to be noted that Jesus regarded prayer as something which is taken for granted in the life of a believer. He said, "When thou prayest," not "if." Prayer is indeed the Christian's vital breath and native air. Once again our Lord denounced ostentatious piety, religious exercises performed for the benefit of onlookers.

The hypocrite plays at prayer. He is never himself, he is always acting a part. Instead of praying behind a closed door to his Father who is in secret, he strikes a pose at the street corner. His object is to draw the attention of the passerby rather than to gain the ear of God. His main aim is to gain a reputation for piety. When men have said of him, "What a holy man," he has already had all the reward that is coming to him (v. 5).

Jesus was not illustrating the relative virtues of public and private prayer, but of sincere versus insincere praying. He then gave the disciples a model prayer which has become popularly known as the Lord's Prayer—the most commonly used liturgical formula in the Christian church. It has, however, lost much of its value because of two abuses. First, its frequent and formal use has often resulted in its becoming vain repetition. Second, its use has been confined practically to public gatherings. Its recitation becomes very formal and leaves little time for meditation on its deep significance.

As if to correct these abuses, Jesus gave two warnings: "When thou prayest, enter into thy closet, and when thou hast shut thy door, pray to thy Father which is *in secret*" (v.

6). "When ye pray, use not *vain repetitions*, as the heathen do: for they think that they shall be heard for their much speaking" (v. 7). He would have them know that the model prayer He was teaching them could easily degenerate into vain repetition, through constant and thoughtless recitation, little better than the Tibetan prayer wheel. The mere repetition of the words has no potency. They are no magical formula. They achieve something only when accompanied by intelligent faith, so the believer who uses the prayer must guard against it becoming a mere mumbled jargon of words.

Then He indicated that the prayer was not only for use on public occasions. It was to be used in secret prayer to the Father. And yet how many of us use this wonderful prayer in secret? There is a striking contrast between the prayer of the Pharisee and the Lord's Prayer (Luke 18:9–14). Instead of praying to the Father, he prayed "with himself." His prayer was offered not in secret but in public. Its content was a complacent review of his own virtues rather than worship and definite petition. Unlike the comprehensiveness of the model prayer, his was characterized by narrow egotism. His arrogant contempt of the publican was the antithesis of the Lord's Prayer.

In teaching the prayer to His disciples, our Lord did not say, "In these words pray ye" but, "After this manner pray ye." He was not laying down an exact formulary, but exemplifying the underlying spiritual principles of prayer. The same principles could be couched in different words.

The prayer has many unique features. Think of its *comprehensiveness*. It covers every aspect of prayer and every area of human need. Consider its *universality*. It is appropriate to the needs of men and women of every race and culture. It is the only religious formulary capable of being translated into every known language. It has a beautiful *simplicity* which can make it meaningful to the youngest and to the illiterate. And yet never has prayer been so *profound*. Its thoughts rove eternity. Perhaps its most remarkable feature is its *brevity*. Were ever any other sixty-five words freighted with such tremendous thoughts and conceptions?

The true spirit in which prayer is to be offered to God is seen in the prayer. We are to pray in an *unselfish* spirit. It is "Our Father," not "My Father." Ours is to be a *filial* spirit, the approach of a son to a father. The prayer is to be offered in a *reverent* spirit: "Hallowed be thy name"; in a *loyal* spirit: "Thy kingdom come"; in a *submissive* spirit: "Thy will be done on earth"; in a *dependent* spirit: "Give us this day our daily bread"; in a *penitent* spirit: "Forgive us our debts"; in a *forgiving* spirit: "As we forgive forgive our debtors"; In a *humble* spirit: "Lead us not into temptation, but deliver us from evil"; in a *triumphant* spirit: "Thine is the kingdom, and the power"; in an *exultant* spirit: "Thine is . . . the glory, for ever."

The prayer embraces every relationship. Child and father: "Our Father"; worshiper and God: "Hallowed be thy name"; subject and king: "Thy kingdom come"; servant and master: "Thy will be done"; beggar and benefactor: "Give us"; pilgrim and guide: "Lead us."

There is a striking symmetry in its structure. It com-mences with an invocation and concludes with a doxology; between these are six petitions. The first three are directed

Godward and for His glory; the last three are manward and concern his need.

There is a missionary slant to the prayer. As we use it in secret, we will ask that His name may be hallowed throughout the whole world. We will pray that His kingdom will know no frontiers. We will petition that His will may be done throughout the whole earth.

Here then is the model of the *manner* in which we are to pray, rather than the exact form we are to use. It is capable of endless expansion. Is anything excluded from it that would add to God's glory or would more completely meet man's need? As we thus pray we have the glorious assurance that our Father who seeth in secret will reward us openly.

SPIRITUAL SELF-DENIAL (VV. 16–19)

Once again our Lord assumed that fasting would be a normal accompaniment of the Christian life. "*When* ye fast." Jesus did not speak against fasting itself, but against the ostentation which robbed it of any true spiritual value. The Pharisees misconceived the principle underlying fasting. Their method of doing it was a misrepresentation of God's attitude. Wearing sackcloth and ashes and disfiguring themselves afforded God no pleasure. Jesus expressed His desire that their joy might be full. While the fasting of the Pharisees may have disciplined their bodies, it fostered their pride and self-complacency.

Fasting in the biblical sense is partial or complete abstinence from food for a period for a spiritual reason. Jesus observed such fasting Himself (Matt. 4:2). In this passage He instructed His disciples concerning the spirit in which it was to be undertaken. It was to be secret, not to be seen of men. It was to be joyous, so that the joy of their service to God might be evident. There is no merit in fasting, per se. But Jesus abstained from appointing any fast as part of His religion (Matt. 9:14; 11:18–19). While not abolishing fasting, He lifted it out of the legalism of the old covenant into the liberty of the new.

In a penetrating study of the subject, Dr. Henry W. Frost asserts that fasting is nowhere enjoined upon the Christian. We may or may not fast as we choose. It is not a legalistic requirement but a spontaneous reaction under special circumstances. Some godly people have found fasting a hindrance rather than a help to prayer. They are so constituted that the lack of a minimum of food renders them unable to concentrate in prayer. There is no need for such to be in bondage. Dr. O. Hallesby observes that fasting is an outward act which should be carried out only when there is an inner need for it.

The idea that food produces carnality while abstinence from food induces spirituality has no biblical support. It is true that overindulgence in food is not conducive to deep spirituality, but that is another matter. Paul taught that "meat commendeth us not to God: for neither, if we eat, are we the better; neither, if we eat not, are we the worse" (1 Cor. 8:8). Clearly, fasting is a matter in which there is complete liberty. And yet it is true that prayer with fasting has been the practice of many great saints—Luther, Baxter, Whitefield, Edwards, Brainerd, Martyn, Hudson Taylor,

Praying Hyde, to mention only a few. It is a practical acknowledgment of the ascendancy of the spiritual. Those who practice it from right motives and in the way suggested by our Lord in this passage, testify to an increased power of concentration on spiritual things. Missionaries have also found that fasting and prayer have triumphed in impossible situations when every other method has failed.

Scriptural teaching would appear to be not that fasting is a carnal means of attaining a spiritual end but that it is the natural outcome of preoccupation. In the New Testament, fasting is nowhere premeditated or prearranged. Historically, it was usually associated with some strong emotion begotten by some spiritual concern. For example, the Lord's temptation (Matt. 4:2); Cornelius beseeching God for a revelation of His truth (Acts 10:30–31); the Antioch leaders burdened for a lost world (Acts 13:1–3); Paul and Barnabas concerned about appointing elders over the infant churches of Asia (Acts 14:23). In the grip of an overmastering concern, these men were led to a prolongation of prayer which precluded the taking of food. The length of time was determined not by previous resolution but by the pressure of the heart concern. When the burden lifted, the fasting ceased.

The key question in each of these spiritual exercises is "Are we content with the approbation of Him who sees in secret, or are we looking mainly for the praise of men?" We are to beware of seeking a spiritual reputation or publishing our spiritual successes and self-denials.

13

More Aspects of Prayer

We know not what we
should pray for as we ought.

ROMANS 8:26

The Spirit-filled Christian is essentially a man of prayer,
since he is indwelt by the Spirit of prayer. In no spiritual
exercise is he more dependent on the Spirit than in his
prayer life.

Prayer is a paradox. No spiritual exercise is such a blending of complexity and simplicity. It is the simplest form
of speech that infant lips can try, yet the sublimest strains
that reach the Majesty on high. It is as appropriate to the
aged philosopher as to the child. It is the ejaculation of a
moment and the attitude of a lifetime. It is the expression
of the rest of faith and of the fight of faith. It is an agony
and an ecstasy. It is submissive and yet importunate. In one
moment it lays hold of God and binds the devil. It can be
focused on a single objective and it can roam the world. It

invests puny man with a sort of omnipotence, for "all things are possible to him that believeth."

Small wonder, then, that even its greatest exponent was forced to admit: "We do not even know how we ought to pray." But he hastens to add: "The Spirit comes to the aid of our weakness . . . through our inarticulate groans the Spirit himself is pleading for us, and God who searches our inmost being knows what the Spirit means, because he pleads for God's own people in God's own way" (Rom. 8:26–27 NEB). He links Himself with us in our praying and pours His supplications into our own.

PRAYER AND THE SPIRIT

With such an encouraging assurance before us, it is clear that in any consideration of the subject of prayer, the Holy Spirit must have prime place. We may master the technique of prayer and understand its philosophy; we may have implicit confidence in the veracity of the promises concerning prayer and spend much time pleading them; but if we consciously or unconsciously ignore the part played by the Holy Spirit, we have failed to use the master key that has been made available to us.

We need constant instruction in the art of praying, and He is the Master Teacher of this basic element of the spiritual life. It is worthy of note that the Spirit's assistance in prayer is more frequently mentioned than any of His other offices. All true praying springs from His activity in the heart. Both Paul and Jude teach that effective prayer is "praying in the Holy Spirit," which has been defined as praying "along the same lines, about the same things, in the same Name as the Holy Spirit." All true prayer rises in the spirit of the believer from the Spirit who indwells him.

Praying in the Spirit may have a dual significance. It may mean praying *in the realm of the Holy Spirit*, for He is the sphere and atmosphere of the believer's life. The Spirit is in us and we are in the Spirit. Many prayers are psychical rather than spiritual. They move in the realm of the mind only, and are the product of our own thinking and not of the Spirit's teaching. But praying in the Spirit is something deeper. The prayer envisaged here "utilizes the body and demands the cooperation of the mind, but moves in the supernatural realm of the Spirit." Prayer conducts its business in the heavenlies.

Or it may mean praying *in the power and energy of the Holy Spirit*: "Give yourselves wholly to prayer and entreaty; pray on every occasion in the power of the Spirit" (Eph. 6:18 neb). Prayer demands more than human power and energy for its supernatural task, and the Holy Spirit supplies it. He is the Spirit of power as well as the Spirit of prayer. Mere human energy of heart and mind and will can achieve only human results. But praying in the power of the Spirit releases supernatural resources.

It is the Spirit's delight to aid us in our physical and moral weakness in the prayer life, for the praying heart labors under three limiting handicaps; but in each of them we can count on the Spirit's assistance. Sometimes we are kept from prayer because of the conscious *iniquity of our hearts*. The Spirit will lead and enable us to appropriate the cleansing of the blood of Christ which will silence the accusations of the adversary and remove the sense of guilt and pollution. Always we are hampered by the limiting *ignorance of our minds*. The Spirit who knows the mind of God will share that knowledge with us as we wait on Him. Then there will come the quiet, clear conviction that our request is in the will of God, and faith will be kindled. We are often earthbound through the benumbing *infirmity of our bodies*. The Spirit will quicken our mortal bodies in response to our faith and enable us to rise above physical and climatic conditions.

Are we availing ourselves of His help along these lines? Is this our present experience? Have we slipped into an independence of the Spirit? Are we habitually praying in the Spirit and receiving full answers to the strategic prayers He inspires? Our intellectual appreciation of spiritual truths often outruns our practical experience of their benefits and implications.

PRAYER AND TIME

Mastering the art of praying in the Spirit will take time, a commodity of which there seems to be a universal and chronic shortage. Lack of time is a much overworked excuse for neglect of duty. And yet, strangely enough, even in the midst of an exacting routine, we always contrive to find time for what we really want to do. In reality, the fundamental problem does not lie in the time factor but in the realm of will and desire. Each of us has all the time there is, and each has as much time as any other. We all choose our own priorities and put first that which we consider most important. If prayer is meager, it is because we consider it supplemental and not fundamental in our program. To our Lord it was not a reluctant addendum but an absolute necessity.

Our Lord moved through life with majestic and measured tread, never in a hurry although always in haste. Thronged with demanding crowds, He always found time to complete His appointed task. Time exercised no power over Him because He knew there were sufficient hours to fulfill His Father's will. If daylight hours afforded insufficient time for prayer, there were always the night hours. And He could always rise "a great while before day" to enjoy the communion with His Father for which there was no other time.

If we trust Him, the Holy Spirit will guide us in allocating sufficient time to prayer and will enable us to do it. Crowding duties also constitute a reason for reducing time spent in prayer. To Martin Luther, extra work was a strong argument for devoting more time to prayer. Once, when asked his plans for the following day, he answered: "Work, work from early to late. In fact, I have so much to do that I shall spend the first three hours in prayer." It all depends on our allocation of priorities.

PRAYER AND SATAN

Prayer is spiritual warfare. "We wrestle . . . against principalities [and] powers." In this aspect of prayer there are three and not two personalities involved. Between God and Satan stands the praying man. Though pitifully weak in himself, he occupies a strategic role in the deathless struggle between the Lamb and the dragon. His power and authority in this warfare are not inherent but derived from the victorious Christ to whom he is united by faith.

Throughout the Gospels, Jesus is seen occupied not so much with the wicked men and evil conditions He confronted as with the forces of evil behind them. Behind the well-meaning Peter and the traitorous Judas, He saw the black hand of Satan. We see souls bound in sin, but our objective in prayer should be not only to pray *for* them but also to pray *against* Satan who holds them captive. He must first be compelled to relax his hold on them, and only the power of Christ's cross appropriated by the prayer of faith can achieve this. Jesus dealt with the cause, not the effect. Do we adopt the same method in our praying?

In a graphic illustration Jesus likened Satan to a well-armed king who, by reason of his power, kept his palace and his goods in peace (Matt. 12:28–29). Before he could be dislodged and his captives released, Jesus said he must himself first be bound and rendered powerless. Only then could the rescue be effected.

What does it mean to bind the strong man, if not to restrain his power by drawing on the conquering power of Him who was manifested to destroy (render inoperative or powerless) the works of the devil (1 John 3:8)? And how is this effected but by the prayer of faith which lays hold on the victory of Calvary and believes for the manifestation in the specific context of the prayer? Let us not make the mistake of reversing the Lord's order and expect to effect the rescue of the captives without first binding the adversary.

Let us confidently accept our divinely given privilege and exercise the authority placed in our hands. "Behold, I have given you authority . . . over all the power of the enemy" (Luke 10:19 RV).

"Satan dreads nothing but prayer," wrote Samuel Chadwick. "The one concern of the devil is to keep the saints from praying. He fears nothing from prayerless studies, prayerless work, prayerless religion. He laughs at our toil, mocks our wisdom, but trembles when we pray."

PRAYER AS LABOR

Both our Lord and Paul made it clear that prayer is no mere pleasant, dreamy reverie. "All vital praying makes a drain on a man's vitality," wrote J. H. Jowett. "True intercession is a sacrifice, a bleeding sacrifice." Jesus performed many mighty works without outward sign of strain, but of His praying it is recorded that "he . . . offered up prayers and supplications with strong crying and tears" (Heb. 5:7).

"Epaphras . . . is always wrestling for you in his prayers," wrote Paul to the Colossian Christians (4:12 MLB). How pale a reflection of Epaphras' intercessions are our languid prayers. The word "wrestling" is that from which our word "agony" is derived. It is used of a man toiling at his work until utterly weary (Col. 1:29), or competing in the arena for the coveted laurel wreath (1 Cor. 9:25). It describes the soldier battling for his life (1 Tim. 6:12), or a man struggling to deliver his friend from danger (John 18:36). It pictures the agony of earnestness of a man to save his own soul (Luke 13:24). But its supreme significance appears in the tragedy of Gethsemane. "Being in an agony he prayed more earnestly" (Luke 22:44), an agony induced by His identification with and grief over the sins of a lost world. Prayer is evidently a strenuous spiritual exercise which demands the utmost mental discipline and concentration. Was it because of this fact that our Lord sometimes linked prayer with fasting?

True intercession is costly. Jesus first gave Himself and then made intercession for His murderers. He could do no more for them. Are we asking of God something we ourselves could supply? Can it be true intercession until we are empty-handed? True intercession demands the sacrifice and dedication of all; it cannot be costless and crossless.

UNANSWERED PRAYER

The fact is that a great many prayers go unanswered, and it is much easier to fatalistically regard unanswered prayer as the will of God than to deliberately set out to discover the causes of failure. Should we be less honest in our approach to this perplexing problem than a merchant to his adverse balance sheet? Perhaps our reluctance to analyze our failures in prayer is rooted in a mistaken solicitude for God's honor. But God is more honored when we ruthlessly face the fact of our unanswered prayers than when we piously ignore it.

The underlying reason for *every* unanswered prayer is that in some way we have asked amiss (James 4:3). Could it be that we have substituted faith in *prayer* for faith in *God*? We are nowhere exhorted to have faith in prayer, but we are counseled, "Have faith in God" (Mark 11:22). Faced with this very problem, the disciples asked Jesus: "Why could we not . . . ?" "Because of your unbelief," replied the Master. An analysis of our prayers might result in the disconcerting discovery that many of them are not the *prayer of faith* at all, but only the prayer of *hope*—or even of *despair*. We earnestly hope that they will be answered, but we have no unshakable assurance to that effect. God has, however, undertaken to answer only the prayer of faith. "Whatever you pray for and ask, believe that you have got it and you shall have it" (Mark 11:24 MOFFATT). Don't think the translator has got his tenses wrong! It is we who have our attitude wrong.

Another prolific source of defeat in prayer is a secret sympathy with sin. "If I regard [cling to] iniquity in my heart, the Lord will not hear me" (Ps. 66:18). Then let us search out and rectify the causes of our unanswered petitions, and the answers will surely come.

14

Let Us Stop Criticizing

One of the perils of the spiritual life is a critical and censorious spirit. It is one of the most serious sins of the
Christian worker, and drew the strictures of our Lord.
The Spirit-filled Christian's speech is characterized by
love.

"Each of us then will have to answer for himself to God.
So let us stop criticizing one another" (Rom. 14:12–13
MOFFATT). This paragraph of Scripture emphasizes the folly
and futility of the critical spirit which not infrequently creeps
into Christian circles. Were we to direct our critical faculty
upon ourselves in view of our inevitable appearance before
the judgment seat of Christ, we would have little inclination
to exercise it on our brother.

One of the tragic evidences of the fall of man is seen in
the fact that most of us are more ready to expose the faults of
others than to extol their virtues. The sin of criticism (using
the word in its secondary sense of finding fault) is very
common among Christian workers. Indeed, is it too much

to say that it is one of the major sins of the church? It does not appear so loathsome as drunkenness or immorality, yet the strictures our Lord passed on such sins of the spirit were far more devastating than those on sins of the flesh. Perhaps there is need for us to revise our standard of values.

From his mother, Augustine learned the evil of criticism and gossip. In order to prevent his dinner-table conversation from degenerating to that level, he had a couplet carved on it. When occasion arose he sometimes drew the attention of his guests to it, to their great embarrassment.

> Who loves another's name to stain,
> He must not dine with me again.

In the course of normal living, it is necessary for us at times to exercise our God-given critical faculty, for criticism, in the primary sense of the word, is neutral. It is the purpose for which we use that faculty and the manner in which we express its findings that determine the moral quality of our words. It can be good or bad according to the spirit in which it is uttered. We are not to be blind to moral or spiritual evil in others, but we must beware of harboring a censorious spirit. Censorious criticism is always flattering to ourselves because it is always delivered from a position of superiority.

In His Sermon on the Mount, our Lord described three types of criticism and, as Archbishop Harrington C. Lees helpfully pointed out, enunciated three related laws:

DESTRUCTIVE CRITICISM

"Judge not, that ye be not judged. For with what judgment ye judge, ye shall be judged: and with what measure ye mete, it shall be measured to you again" (Matt. 7:1–2). The word "judge" here carries the idea of discriminating or distinguishing and does not necessarily have a bad connotation. Our judging could result in either approval or condemnation, but taken in its context it bears the latter meaning. It is the habit of censorious, sharp, unjust criticism that is in view. This was the sin of the Pharisee who used the publican as a backdrop to display his superior virtue. This is no Christian activity and must be permanently and decisively stopped. In this statement Jesus was not "warning His disciples of a possible danger but forbidding an actual habit already indulged." This is indicated by the tense of the verb. Paul gives the same authoritative and categorical injunction: "Let us not therefore judge one another any more" (Rom. 14:13).

There are valid reasons for this decisive command of Christ. At best our knowledge is only partial. We do not and cannot know all the facts. We see the issue but are ignorant of the factors involved. We see the fall before temptation, but who can measure the full force of that temptation, or the degree of hidden resistance before the fall? We form our judgment from superficial knowledge drawn from external appearances. Only God knows all the facts, therefore only He can reach a true judgment.

There is sound wisdom in the legal maxim that an *ex parte* statement should never be accepted without checking.

There is always another side to every case. If we possessed all the facts, we would indulge in less harsh criticism.

Then, too, at best our judgment is fallible. Even if we did know all the facts, that would not ensure our interpreting them correctly. Two people can be presented with the same set of facts and arrive at exactly opposite conclusions. This constantly happens when a jury, having heard the same evidence and addresses, fails to agree. We must therefore be merciful in our judgments. It is not for us to usurp God's throne of judgment or pass a final verdict.

THE LAW OF RETRIBUTION

Censorious criticism is a boomerang which rebounds on the one who indulges in it. "With what judgment ye judge, ye shall be judged." This is illustrated by the law of dynamics, that action and reaction are equal and opposite. The blow we strike at any object will recoil upon us with the force of our stroke. Our unloving criticism will return on our own heads. The measuring tape we use for gauging the faults of others will be the measure used by both God and man on our own conduct. "Thou wicked servant," said Jesus, "out of thine own mouth will I judge thee" (Luke 19:22).

Scripture is replete with illustrations of this law. With poetic justice the wicked Haman was hanged on the very gallows he had erected for Mordecai. When Adoni-bezek was captured and punished by the Israelites, he said: "Threescore and ten kings, having their thumbs and their great toes cut off, gathered their food under my table: as I have done, so God hath requited me" (Judges 1:7 ASV).

There is another though less important reason why we should stop criticizing. Nothing will make our company less welcome to right-thinking people. Greek mythology had its Momus, the god of criticism, who lived on Mount Olympus with the other gods. He always found something to criticize, no matter how loud others were in their praise.

Jupiter, Minerva, and Neptune once had a competition to see who could make the most perfect thing. Jupiter made a man, Neptune a bull, and Minerva a house. When the gods were invited to pass judgment, Momus found fault with all three; with the man, because he had no window in his breast through which the thoughts of his soul might be read; with the bull, because its horns were not below its eyes so that he might see when he butted with them; with the house, because it was not on wheels, so that it could be removed from bad neighbors. So unpopular did Momus become that the other gods banished him from Mount Olympus.

DELUDED CRITICISM

"And why beholdest thou the mote that is in thy brother's eye . . .? Thou hypocrite, first cast out the beam out of thine own eye; and then shalt thou see clearly to cast out the mote out of thy brother's eye" (Matt. 7: 3, 5).

With unerring perception Jesus exposed the insincerity of much criticism. Those who are lynx-eyed in detecting small defects in others are often quite blind to their own greater faults. A passion to put others right may very well be suspect in the light of this counsel. "A blind guide is bad enough," wrote Alexander Maclaren, "but a blind oculist is a still more ridiculous anomaly." Our criticism is so often wrong because our moral vision is blurred by our own faults.

Were it not so true to life, the illustration of the beam, large enough to make a rafter, and the mote, a tiny speck of sawdust, would be ludicrous. So very often we have in our own characters a much larger edition of the defect we see so clearly in others. The jealous person is quick to impute jealousy to others, for he himself would be jealous under similar circumstances. The merciless critic has no right to condemn another while oblivious to his own shortcomings.

Jesus had in view the removal of both the beam and the mote, but He was saying that before we are qualified for the delicate task of removing the speck from our brother's eye, we must first deal with the plank in our own. It is often the man who is guilty of large dishonest practice in his own business who is most severe on petty theft among his employees.

THE LAW OF RESTRAINT

It was in this connection that Jesus enunciated the law of restraint. Before we adversely criticize another, we should first engage in healthy self-criticism lest it be said of us, "Therefore thou art inexcusable, O man, whosoever thou art that judgest: for wherein thou judgest another, thou condemnest thyself; for thou that judgest doest the same things" (Rom. 2:1). Honest self-criticism will restrain from censorious criticism of others and will save us from the judgment of God (1 Cor. 11:31).

Praying Hyde of India learned a lesson which he said was the most salutary the Lord ever taught him. He was burdened about the spiritual condition of a certain pastor and resolved to spend time in intercession for him. He began pouring out his heart for him somewhat as follows: "O God, Thou knowest this brother, how—" He was going to say "cold," when suddenly a hand seemed to be laid on his lips, and a voice said to him in stern reproach: "He that toucheth him toucheth the apple of mine eye." A great horror came over Hyde. He had been guilty before God of "accusing the brethren." He had been judging his brother. He fell to his knees rebuked and humbled. It was he himself who first needed putting right. He confessed his sin and claimed cleansing. "Whatsoever things . . . are lovely . . . [and] of good report . . . think on these things" (Phil. 4:8). Then he cried, "Father, show me what things are lovely and of good report in my brother's life." Like a flash, he remembered how that pastor had given up all for Christ and endured much suffering. He was reminded of years of hard work, of the tact with which he had managed a difficult congregation, of the many quarrels he had healed, of what a model husband he was. And so all his prayer session was spent in praise for his brother instead of prayer.

When Mr. Hyde went down to the plains, he found that just then the pastor had received a great spiritual uplift. While he was praising, God had been blessing. We must guard against our prayers for others degenerating into oblique criticism. "Cast out the beam out of thine own eye," get the passion for criticism removed, and then you will see clearly not the mote but how to remove it.

DISCRIMINATING CRITICISM

"Give not that which is holy unto the dogs, neither cast ye your pearls before swine, lest they trample them under their feet, and turn again and rend you" (Matt. 7:6). The same Jesus who said, "Judge not" also said, "Judge righteous judgment" (John 7:24). In saying this He did not contradict Himself. There is a permissible and necessary criticism as well as a forbidden one. We must learn to discriminate between people and regulate our behavior in the light of our judgment.

Christ uses "dogs" and "swine" as typical of certain classes of people—obviously unholy people. In the Orient, dogs were frequently repulsive and foul scavengers. Our Lord apparently had in mind the ravenous gorging of a dog on the flesh of the holy burnt offering. The sacred character of the food meant nothing to the dog. Swine, too, were unclean animals and to the Jew, eating swine's flesh was an abomination.

The terms are clearly used of those who are *not* Christians. Christians are called "sheep." The priests were not to throw the part of the sacrifice reserved for them to the filthy dogs. Pearls were not to be thrown to swine, who had no appreciation of them but might mistake them for beans and, finding themselves cheated, would trample the gems and rend the giver.

Spiritual treasures are not to be shared with those who

have no appreciation of them. While we are not to be destructively critical, we should exercise discernment and discrimination in our dealings with men. The materialist has little appreciation of the spiritual. There are glorious truths which can be apprehended only by the spiritual man. There are some spiritual experiences so intimate and personal that "their bloom would pass in the telling." If we are wise, we will be selective in those with whom we share the deeps of our hearts or the sacred things of the Word. Even our Lord shared truth with His disciples only "as they were able to bear it." While we must not judge our fellows lightly or hastily, when a man has displayed his true character, we should be careful what we say to him. This counsel of our Lord authorizes us to employ a sensible and discriminating criticism, and this divinely illumined power of criticism will enable us to discern what is fitting for those to whom we speak.

THE LAW OF RETICENCE

Our divine Master practiced His own precepts. When He was taken to Herod, the king "was exceeding . . . glad [and] questioned with him in many words; but he answered him nothing." Jesus refused to give that which was holy to dogs, or to cast His pearls before swine. He observed the law of reticence. It is for us to follow His example.

"There are times when Christian silence is more to be commended than Christian loquacity in the presence of folks who are morally and spiritually incapable of appreciation," said H. C. Lees.

Bible Study for Personal Profit

Thy words were found, and I did eat them.

JEREMIAH 15:16

We are counseled to let the word of Christ dwell in us richly. The degree in which we do this will determine our growth and stability and maturity in the spiritual life.

In treating this subject, the full inspiration of the Scriptures is taken for granted. With our whole hearts we believe it to be not only God's Word but God's Word to us (1 Thess. 2:13). We believe that it has relevance not only to our times but to our lives. We believe that through it God reveals general principles and also truth appropriate to our changing needs. We believe that it is admirably adapted to make the man of God perfect and mature in character, and to equip him for every good work (2 Tim. 3:16–17). With this background of conviction we can proceed to consider how we may study the Bible that these two ends may be secured. What is written here will be familiar ground to many, but a rethinking of familiar truths can be helpful.

In our Bible study it is too easy to read with a view to the profit of others for whom we have spiritual responsibility, but we must reserve a time when we read selfishly, for our own profit. It will benefit others later. Devotional Bible study differs from exegetical study, but the latter should not be neglected. The nurture of our own spiritual life is a prime necessity to effective service. Now we are alone with God. He speaks to us through His Word. We speak to Him in prayer. It is a two-way conversation. This is communion, when we share with God what we have in common in Christ, who is the center of Scripture. Where will we meet the Lord and commune with Him? At the mercy seat. "There I will meet with thee, and I will commune with thee from above the mercy seat" (Ex. 25:22).

OUR OBJECTIVE

The supreme knowledge is the knowledge of God in Christ, and to know Him more perfectly is the aim of our devotional Bible study. Every highway and byway in Scripture leads to Christ. In Him all promises and predictions are fulfilled. He is the key that unlocks the secrets of the Book. Directly or indirectly all Scripture leads to His Person and work, His mission and offices, His two advents, the consummation of all in His coming kingdom. If we fail to find Him in the Old Testament, it becomes merely interesting religious literature.

THE APPROACH

Use a Bible without divisions or notes so that your thoughts do not automatically run into old molds. Leave it open to the Holy Spirit to flash fresh light on the page.

Have another version by you to stimulate thought. Long familiarity with the words of a loved version tends to render them commonplace and innocuous.

Read the portion to find out exactly what it says. One of the milestones in D. L. Moody's career came when he decided to find out what the Bible *said*, not first what it *meant*. This is not so elementary as it may appear.

Read broadly in the Bible, not favorite devotional portions only, not only those which are comforting. God speaks to us as really in His warnings and rebukes as in His encouragements. At times our personal profit is secured better by a shattering word than a comforting one.

Read expectantly, constantly in the attitude, "What saith my Lord to his servant?"

THE ART OF MEDITATION

The blessed man of Psalm 1 is the man who meditates in the Word day and night. Meditation is not dreamy reverie. It is concentration of mind on the thoughts of God, depending on the Holy Spirit for enlightenment. It is a spiritual chewing of the cud. "Thy words were found, and I did eat them," said Jeremiah (15:16). This illustration is very apposite. We break off a piece of bread and masticate it until it can be swallowed. It is then cared for by the gastric juices and becomes part of our physical constitution, transmuted into blood, bone, muscle—and even thought and speech. How? That is a mystery to the uninitiated, but we do not stumble at it. We just reach for another piece of bread.

So with meditation. Take a small passage, or even a word, and think on it. Ask yourself questions about it; recall other related passages; turn it into prayer, remembering that God is speaking to you in it. When this process of mental mastication is complete, the Holy Spirit—we know not how—takes the thoughts on which we have meditated and incorporates them into our spiritual life. We have been fed with the Bread of Life, Christ Himself.

As a simple example, take Psalm 23:1. Meditate on "shepherd." Think of all the Eastern shepherd is to his sheep. Next, "the Lord." Allow your mind to dwell on His greatness, holiness, love, care, power, His self-expression in Christ. Next, "my." Join the two thoughts and worship so great a God who sustains such a relationship to you. Then, "is"—at this very moment. He is and always will be my Shepherd.

TURNING SCRIPTURE INTO PRAYER

As an inspired prayer book, the Bible is a great stimulus to the life of worship and devotion. The Psalms, for example, strike every note in the whole range of human experience. There is something to match every mood and meet every situation; to kindle inspiration and inspire faith; to stimulate worship and encourage intercession. For this reason it is wise to have Bible reading before your time of prayer. In turning a psalm into prayer, apply it to your present situation and need. The psalmist's physical foes become your spiritual enemies. Use his inspired words as the expression of your own heart. With him, become lost in wonder, love, and praise at the greatness and goodness of God.

Where there is a promise, fulfill the conditions and claim it; a warning, heed it; an example, emulate it; a command, obey it without evasion or delay, for obedience is an essential element in receiving more light. Look for the spiritual principles which, though not formally enunciated, are everywhere present in the Word.

Nothing so feeds the spiritual life as worship. Dr. R. A. Torrey bore testimony to the great transformation which came to him when he learned not only to pray and return thanks but to worship. "Earth has no joy," he wrote, "like that which fills the soul as we bow before God in worship, asking nothing, seeking nothing from Him, occupied with Himself and satisfied with Himself." The Scriptures are rich in material to induce worship. What vast tracts await our exploration and exploitation! What spacious themes—His sovereignty, holiness, mercy, love, faithfulness, patience, grace. When viewed as the unveiling of Jesus Christ rather than the unfolding of future events, the Apocalypse is especially rich in devotional content.

THE USE OF THE IMAGINATION

Dr. W. E. Sangster gives helpful advice on the use of the imagination in Bible study. "The devout student," he writes, "has learned to live in the Bible. By a reverent use of the

imagination, he has developed a method of slipping within
the covers of the Book and making it autobiographical."
He suggests that the noblest use of the imagination is not
to plan things for the future but to run back through the
corridors of time and call up the scenes and facts of our
Lord's life, and to be present as if in body at every recorded
event of the history of the Redeemer; to run back through
time and jostle with Peter and James and John when they
stand around the Savior; to see Lazarus emerging from the
tomb; to sit with Mary at Jesus' feet . . . The proper use of
the imagination is to take true things and make them vivid
in the life of today. We can read the Bible from the outside
or the inside. We can come to it in a detached fashion and
always be external to it, or we can slip between its covers
and live within the divine Word itself. Here is a suggestion
well worth trying out.

THE HOLY SPIRIT

Probably one of the main reasons for not deriving more
personal profit from our Bible study is our often unwitting
failure to accord to the Holy Spirit His place as interpreter
of the Bible. If we approach the Scriptures depending,
consciously or unconsciously, on our human abilities and
equipment, what we derive from them will be largely on
the level of the human. If we read in dependence on the
Holy Spirit, He is pledged to "guide [us] into all truth"
(John 16:13). The unaided mind, William Barclay reminds
us, discovers only partial truth. Even strenuous thinking
unaided by the Holy Spirit can lead to frustration and

bewilderment, for the mind by itself can produce more problems than solutions. Thinking and praying must go hand in hand. The Spirit can give us a flash of illumination and we should expect it.

It is the delight of the Spirit to take of the things of Christ and show them to us (John 16:13). He is the intermediary of Christ and God and speaks to us what He hears from God. He is Christ's remembrancer (John 14:26), and as we rely on His cooperation in our study, He will bring to our remembrance the very verses or truths we need, and at the very moment we need them.

Since this is true, each time we approach the Word for personal profit we should bow and humbly seek His help and illumination.

MORE FROM J. OSWALD SANDERS

Sanders presents and illustrates several magnifying principles through the lives of prolific men. *Spiritual Leadership* will encourage you to place your talents and powers at God's disposal so you can become a leader used for His glory.

978-0-8024-1670-4

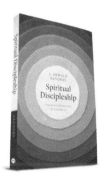

True discipleship is more than intellectual assent to a belief in Christ; it involves the whole person and lifestyle. This book will help you embody that truth. It examines Jesus' teaching on what it means to follow Him, helping you become the kind of Christian Jesus wants you to be—not one devised by man or even other Christians.

978-0-8024-1669-8

Spiritual maturity is not a level of growth Christians achieve, but the passion to press on in Christ. In this book, J. Oswald Sanders provides clear direction for those desiring to grow strong spiritually. Complete with scriptural principles for spiritual development and study questions at the end of the text, this classic handbook is a timeless treasure.

978-0-8024-1671-1

MOODY
Publishers®

From the Word to Life®

also available as eBooks

A
Spiritual
Clinic

J. Oswald
Sanders

MOODY
Publishers

From the Word to Life

We all go through seasons of fatigue that take their toll, and we can easily fall into apathy. Sanders prescribes a powerful tonic of scriptural principles that lead to recovery and growth. Perfect for anyone who feels worn out from their Christian life and could use a little spiritual doctoring.

978-0-8024-1889-0 | also available as an eBook

BRINGING YOU *timeless classics*

Selected for their enduring excellence and timeless perspective, these are key books that every believer on the journey of spiritual formation should read.

MOODY Publishers®

From the Word to Life®

DO YOU LONG TO BE MORE LIKE CHRIST?

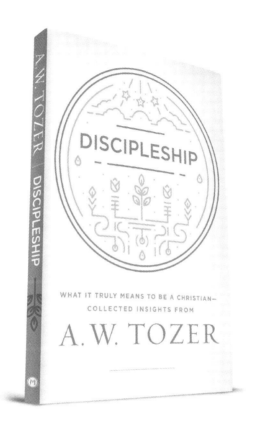

WHAT IT TRULY MEANS TO BE A CHRISTIAN—
COLLECTED INSIGHTS FROM

A. W. TOZER